I0540021

The Diary of a Dope Fiend's Daughter

A journey through substance abuse: From hurt to healing

LaTanya Beasley-Carter

Table of Contents

DEDICATION

To my mother, who will celebrate 27 years of sobriety in July 2025. Your fight became our foundation. Your healing gave me room to grow.

To my father, the late Raymond Earl Dotson (passed 2021), who found his strength the day after I told him he couldn't walk me down the aisle as an addict. He did the work in his way. He got clean enough to walk me down that aisle in 2019, full of pride. He may be gone, but he walked me and that will always matter.

To my late Granny, Louvenia Beasley (1/19/03), and my Aunt Priscilla "Cil" Dotson (1/24/04). Two amazing women who tagged-teamed and stepped in when my mother and father couldn't show up emotionally or financially. They reminded me I could still be loved and supported, even when my parents were unavailable.

To my late grandmother, Margella Dotson, who showed me love and care long before I even knew I needed it.

To my late uncle, Robert "Bobby" Beasley, "the Tickle Monster". He was the first to warn me about the dangers of substance abuse, how addiction sneaks up, and how his own addiction became his downfall.

PREFACE

This book is for the child who had to grow up too fast.
The one who was forced to carry shame that didn't belong to them.
The one who held on to secrets that felt too heavy, too confusing,
too much.

It's for the adult they became.
The one who's still trying to make sense of it all.
Still learning how to heal from what they survived.
Still figuring out how to parent themselves, while maybe raising
kids of their own.

It's also for the parent or caregiver who didn't get it right.
The one who caused harm, whether they meant to or not.
The one who's trying now... trying to face the past, do the work, or
just understand what it looked like through their child's eyes.

Diary of a Dope Fiend's Daughter isn't just about addiction.
It's about what it does to a home, to a child, to a life. This is a story
about memory, rage, forgiveness, grief, laughter, and love. It's
about what it looks like when you finally decide to speak the truth
out loud.

You might not be that little kid anymore.
But they're still in there.
And they deserve to be seen and heard.

This is my story.
But I hope you find pieces and space of yours in it too.

LaTanya Beasley-Carter

A NOTE ABOUT THE HEART WORK

Before you go any further, I want to tell you about something important in this book. At the end of each chapter, you'll find something I call *The Heart Work*. It's split into two parts.

One is for the adult child of an addict. The one who grew up in the chaos, who may still be sorting through the silence, the pain, or the pieces of a childhood that never felt fully theirs. That part is for you.

The other is for the parent or caregiver in recovery. And even if you're not there yet, if you're still figuring it out or unsure what recovery even looks like, but you're holding this book in your hands anyway... that's a start

You don't have to write your answers. But if you do, let them be honest. Even if it's messy or uncomfortable. You're not doing this to impress anyone. You're doing it to heal.

Wherever you are, let this meet you there. No pressure to be further along. No shame for still working through it.

Just begin.

The fact that you're here means... you already have.

INTRODUCTION

I didn't grow up journaling.
I grew up writing in diaries that I hid in ceiling cracks.

To save my sanity, I wrote poems.

In the '90s, poetry wasn't about being crafty. In my world, writing
poetry was about getting something out before it ate me alive.
I wrote wherever I could, whenever I could. In spiral notebooks or
on the backs of late bills.
My poems weren't polished. They were a kind of survival. And they
were often misunderstood.

I couldn't always speak what I felt.
But I could write what I felt, in my safe space, alone.

That's what poetry was for me. A private place where my words
gave me a soft and melodic voice in a world full of chaos.

That's what this is. A space for your words and your stories.

The ones you replay in your head.
The ones you know you need to release but never knew how.

The words you write here don't need to be cleaned up for anyone.
They just need to come out, so you can finally name what you've
been holding sacred.

The Diary of a Dope Fiend's Daughter came from those same late-
night scribbles. The parts of my story I didn't hold in shame, but

sometimes kept in my head because I never had the space or the courage to say them out loud.

This isn't a guide.
I pray it's a healing process and a place to let it all out.

If you were raised in homes where people mastered the art of being present one moment and nodding off the next...
If you know what it means to live on broken promises...
If writing is the only place you've ever felt safe, or you've never been given a safe space at all...

Then this is for you.

You don't owe anyone a neat story. You just owe yourself the truth. And some of us owe our parents, our adult children, and others our true, unfiltered story.

You made it here and that's not small.
That's a huge step in the direction of healing.

Even if you don't write another word, know this...
sometimes showing up to the page is the first step.

Let's write what's next.

LaTanya
Wife. Mother. Woman of God. Poet. Daughter. Witness. Survivor.

DISCLAIMER

This book contains real-life accounts of trauma, addiction, emotional pain, and suicide. These stories are shared with honesty and vulnerability, and may stir strong emotions in those reading or reflecting.

Please note:

This is not a clinical tool or a substitute for therapy.
This is a space for storytelling, self-reflection, and shared truth.

If at any point you feel overwhelmed, PAUSE. BREATHE. Seek support if it's too much for you.
Healing is not a race and no one can tell you how to do it right.

This book does not assign blame, it does not pass judgement, it offers understanding. It does not demand forgiveness, it offers perspective.

You are free to take what resonates and I ask you to peacefully leave what doesn't.

Move through these pages with care for me, my parents, yourself and those you may share them with.

A Letter To The Parent In Recovery

Dear You,

If you're holding this journal, it means you've decided to look back so you can move forward, and that takes courage.

You may have carried shame for years. You may have believed your child would never forgive you, or that you could never forgive yourself. You may still struggle to understand the weight your addiction placed on your family, or maybe you know it all too well.

If you're reading this, it shows you care and you want to heal. You are here, because you want to give your child, no matter how grown they are now, the version of you they always deserved.

This journal is not about blaming or tearing open old wounds just to bleed again. It's about honesty and accountability. It's about seeing your child's story and letting them see yours without excuses, without defenses, and with a heart willing to listen.

You are not your past, you are not your addiction, and you are allowed to change. You are allowed to show up, even if it's late.

May this be a place where you can unpack your journey, honor your growth, and learn how to be present in your child's healing even if that looks different than you imagined.

Thank you for being here, thank you for trying, you are not alone.

With hope,
LaTanya

A Letter To The Adult Child of Addiction

Dear You,

You didn't deserve the chaos you were born into. You didn't deserve the confusion, the missed moments, or the silence you learned to carry alone. None of it was your fault.

You were just a child. You were allowed to want stability, to crave love that didn't have to compete with a drug, and to wish for a parent who showed up every time they promised they would.

If you're reading this, you're likely not a child anymore. You've grown up and you have found ways to survive, to build a life, and to smile again. I understand there may still be parts of you holding on to anger, grief, and questions you never got to ask.

This journal is designed for you to explore those questions safely, to give words to the feelings you buried to keep moving forward. It's a place to remember what you felt, to honor what you lost, and choose what you want and how you want to heal.

You do not have to forgive if you are not ready. You don't have to make excuses for what happened. You're allowed to feel however you feel and you deserve a space to process it, piece by piece in your own time.

May this be your place to breathe, write, reflect, and to find your voice again. You are not alone. I was there, in a different setting, but with the same storyline.

With love,
LaTanya

HEALING AGREEMENT

Before we go any further, let's make a promise:
This book is a space for honesty, reflection, and growth.
For **you** and for the relationship that may one day be rebuilt.
Healing doesn't mean forgetting what happened.
It doesn't mean forcing forgiveness before you're ready.
It means *choosing* to face the truth, to listen without judgment,
and to work toward a better future.
You don't have to agree on every memory.
You don't have to rush to fix everything in one conversation.
But trying would mean a lot to someone.
If you are using this journal with a parent or adult child:

- Agree to listen before responding.
- Agree to take breaks when emotions feel too heavy.
- Agree to respect each other's truths, even if they're hard to hear.

If you can't sign this agreement right now, that's okay. Healing has no deadline.
You can still start small:

- Send a "How's your day?" text.
- Share a hug once a day.
- Plan a breakfast or dinner together, just to be present.
- Sit in the same room while journaling, even if no words are spoken.

Signature:
I am choosing to show up for myself and for my healing.

Adult Child: _____
Parent: _____

"Forgiveness is giving up the hope that the past could have been any different." — Oprah Winfrey

CHAPTER ONE: Back Down Memory Lane

A therapist, a skyline, and the question
That cracked everything open

In downtown Chicago, one cold winter evening in 1995, we took an elevator to a high floor with a beautiful view of the city. The skyline stretched beyond the glass, buildings glowing under the hum of office lights. Snow flurries scraped softly against the windows, disappearing as quickly as they came.

It was just my mom and me that night. Her boyfriend had driven us there, but he stayed in the lobby. No cell phone to scroll, no earbuds to drown out the waiting. Maybe he was flipping through an old *Essence* or *Jet* magazine. Maybe he just sat there, staring at the floor, waiting for this to be over because it was late in the evening.

I was sixteen, hands shoved deep into the pockets of my winter coat, stomach knotted, but somehow still a little excited to finally get some kind of help. My heart was beating fast, like it already knew something was about to change.

Three weeks earlier, I had written a poem. I'd written plenty before. scribbled in notebooks, shared with friends, written in the margins of homework. But I shared this one with my mom. And in typical "my momma fashion," it passed from one set of hands to another. Whispered about in hushed phone calls. Shared with my aunt, who decided to type it out for me. Eventually, it landed in front of someone who didn't just see another piece of writing. They saw a cry for help.

My aunt's observation led us here.

The therapist's office smelled like lavender and something faintly medicinal, like an old library book, something worn and familiar. She was a Black woman with caramel skin, round cheeks, and a roller set hairstyle that framed her face. Her black blazer and faded red lipstick looked tired, probably from a long day of talking.

I remember her office like a dream I accidentally woke up in. A dark wooden desk with a heavy office chair. An hourglass on the shelf I couldn't stop glancing at. A silver pen resting on a worn leather journal. She sat with her back to the windows, so she couldn't see what I saw — an endless view of the city, Lake Michigan glinting, wrapped in the arms of skyscrapers.

That night, that view became my escape. And to this day, the view of Chicago's skyline still is.

My mom sat beside me, silent. I could feel her tension in the way she crossed and uncrossed her legs, in the careful way she breathed.

The therapist had already read the poem. I could tell by the way she looked at me. She wasn't just waiting, she was expecting me to explain something.

Then she spoke.
"What is your first memory of your mom using drugs?"

The question landed like a weight.

Like, whoa, this lady just came out swinging.

I blinked. Looked at my mom. Then turned back to the window. I sighed.

The poem had said a lot of things, but not that.

Heck, no one had ever asked me to paint the picture of that memory.

The poem...

It hadn't described the missing time, the long stretches of absence behind the bedroom door I had learned not to ask about.

It hadn't painted the picture of strange people passing through our house, voices low.

And it hadn't described the silence. The way my mom's eyes would glaze over and her body would seem to disappear into itself, nodding off right there in the room, gone even though she hadn't left.

I swallowed. My throat was dry. The window blurred, and my reflection ghosted over the lights of the city.

I could lie or say I didn't remember.

But the truth was already there. I had an outlet beyond my pen and paper now, and it was hanging in the silence between us.

And saying it out loud could possibly change everything.

What scared me most wasn't telling the truth. It was the fact that I still had such vivid memories of the first time.

That was the first time anyone asked.

The first time someone looked past my poetry and not only saw the pain behind it, but also offered a helping hand.

That was also the first time my mom sat beside me to hear my story in a safe space. She couldn't get mad, she couldn't put up a defense. She just listened.

Sharing that first memory of her using drugs was the moment that memory stopped hiding.

My memory happened about eleven years prior.

Every detailed memory I gave the therapist introduced her pen to her journal. She didn't interrupt me, and neither did my mom. My mom kept her composure as I gave every detail of such a heavy topic.

For the first time, I realized the words I had written weren't just poems.

The poem?

It deserves its own space.

But this?

This is the story of how what I wrote to express my feelings became the cry for help I didn't know I needed.

Truth Be Told

Truth be told, going back down memory lane isn't always about pain. Sometimes it's about freedom, the kind you don't even realize you need until you finally open your mouth and say what's been sitting heavy on your chest or lying quiet in the back of your mind for years.

That day in the therapist's office, I spoke out loud the things I had only ever written down in poems or said to my mom in frustration. I thought writing it was enough. But saying it, and saying it where my mother could hear it, that was a freedom I didn't even know existed.

Looking back now, going down memory lane helps me see how far I've come. It reminds me my story holds testimony, not just pain. Those memories don't make me sad or angry anymore. They remind me that life changes, and that God protects us, even when the memories try to tear us down.

If you're hesitant to go back down your own memory lane, I understand. But I hope you'll remember this, sometimes what's waiting for you there isn't more pain. Sometimes, freedom is what's waiting for you.

LET'S DO THE HEART WORK

Take your time with these. You don't need perfect sentences, grammar, or a neat story here. This is your space to tell the truth you've been holding. Breathe, pray, and just write. Remember, God can handle your honesty.

The Heart Work For

Adult Children of Addicts

What's the first time someone asked you a question you weren't ready to answer?

- Who asked it, and what was the question?
- How did you feel in your body when it was asked?
- What did you say, and what did you wish you could have said?
- If you could answer that question now, what truth would you speak?

When did you first realize your parent or caregiver wasn't okay?

- How old were you, and what was happening around you?
- What did you see, hear, or feel that let you know something wasn't right?
- What did you do with that realization? Did you tell anyone, or did you keep it inside?
- How does that moment still live in you today?

If someone had read your words when you were younger, your journal, your poetry, your silence what would they have seen?

- What would you have written about back then?
- What did you feel you couldn't write about?
- If someone really saw you in those pages, what would you have wanted them to understand about you?

The Heart Work for Parents in Recovery

What do you wish your child or children knew about your story?

- What was going on in your life when you first started using?
- What pain were you trying to numb?
- What would you want your child or children to know about who you were before addiction?
- What would it mean to share this truth with them one day?

Is there a moment in your parenting that still feels heavy on your heart?

- What happened, and what do you wish had gone differently?
- How does that moment sit in your heart now?
- What have you told yourself about that moment?
- What would it look like to let God help you begin releasing its weight?

What does healing look like for you now?

- What does recovery mean to you beyond sobriety?
- Who do you want to become as you heal?
- What does a "safe space" look like for you now, and how can you create it?
- What would you write in a letter to your child about your healing?

Sometimes the deepest healing comes from being honest about the hurt."
— Unknown

CHAPTER TWO: First Come, First Served

A rotating door, a radiator seat, and a
Child's front-row view of addiction.

It was a rigid, cold winter night in Chicago. The high winds cut through the streets, sending a chill so sharp it made my face ache with every gust. I was about five years old, bundled up in a coat that didn't feel nearly warm enough. My mom and I were on our way back to that building. Not the one from therapy, not somewhere safe. This was a different place. She took me there a few times, right off 67th and Normal, near an elementary school.

It was a dark brick, four-unit building, standing next to a dirty yellow, two-flat-frame house. The building was secured; we always had to be buzzed in. The buzzer was loud, echoing through the stairwell, and by the time we reached the first landing, it would stop.

The hallways smelled like old wood and cheap cigarettes, with dirty carpet on the stairs, dark wooden banisters, and handrails worn smooth from years of gripping hands. Each apartment had a gated entry with security bars and padlocks. We always went to the second floor. Someone was always there, watching, keeping the padlock secure. In hindsight, it was a fire hazard.

At the second floor, Mom slid her hand through the diamond-shaped openings in the rusted grayish-silver gate to knock on the door. The person inside didn't always check the peephole. Sometimes, they just opened the door after a few quick raps, trusting the knock's rhythm more than the person.

Then, we waited.

One by one, the sounds of deadbolt locks clicking open filled the hallway. Clink. Clink. Clink.

After the last one, the door finally creaked open. But even then, we weren't inside yet.

The person on duty shuffled through a ring of keys, searching for the right one to unlock the gate. The metal jingled softly, sliding over itself until the right key clicked, the padlock snapped open, and the gate slid just wide enough for us to squeeze through.

I can still hear that faint creaking sound.

Inside, the apartment was dimly lit, the air thick and stale like smoke and spoiled food. I was told to sit on the radiator in the empty living room. The heat barely worked, but the metal was still warm under my hands as I gripped the edge.

And then, I waited again.

The apartment had an unknown number of bedrooms. The living room had brownish-orange shag carpet, worn flat in some places, with dark spots where feet had rested too long. The only furniture was an old yellow vinyl chair, positioned near the door for whoever was on watch. An ashtray sat beside it, overflowing with cigarette butts and ashes that never seemed to get emptied.

In the connected dining room, an old, scratched-up wooden table sat under a weak bulb. On it were razor blades, small bags of white powder, cut-up straws near a scale, and a beige vintage triple-beam balance pan scale. I took my seat on the radiator by the window, where I could see the door, the dining table (which I'm sure was never used for dining), and the unfriendly, slender man with dark skin and bad acne.

As soon as I sat down, my mom disappeared into what I assumed was a bedroom and the door closed behind her.

I sat patiently on the radiator alone, watching everything I didn't know I would remember years later.

With every knock, the slender man would grab a silver-handled pistol from his waistband, stand, check the peephole, then remove a light wood 2x4 that braced the door shut. Then, he'd go through the same routine: turning the key in one deadbolt, twisting the knob on another, before cracking the door just enough to see who was there.

If they passed his check, he'd let them in. Keys jingling, locks clicking, the gate screeching as it slid open. Once inside, the visitor would head straight to the back, where my mom was.

The cycle repeated. Again and again. First come, first served.

I don't know how long I sat there, but eventually, my mom reappeared.

She tried to be playful by smiling at me. The smile was unauthentic and her eyes were always different when she came out. They were lower, unfocused, and carrying a pain I couldn't understand back then.

And I always remember the powdered residue clinging to the hairs beneath her nose.

That was the moment. The memory. The answer to the therapist's question. The truth I carried in silence until someone finally asked.

Telling that story out loud, sitting across from the therapist with my mother right beside me, felt like pressing on a bruise I had convinced myself didn't hurt anymore.

My mom shifted in her seat, her face tight. I could see her trying to act like it didn't bother her, like it wasn't news. But her leg bounced, and her jaw set tighter the longer I talked. The therapist nodded slowly, introducing her pen to her journal, letting the silence stretch until my own breath sounded too loud in my ears.

The look of embarrassment and shame covered my mom's face. I'm not sure if she was embarrassed that I shared what she thought I didn't remember—or if she felt shame for exposing me to something she thought I had forgotten.

Heck, I wasn't even sure if she remembered my first memory, but I painted the picture as if we were there yesterday.

I didn't cry in that moment. I think my body had learned to save tears for later, when no one was watching. What I did feel was this strange mix of shame and relief. Like opening a window in a room that had been locked for years. Cold air rushing in to give space for the stuffy room to breathe and air out all that had been smothered in my silence.

I can't remember anything else the therapist asked me that day. I only remember the important question. The one that led me to speak about a visit that was etched in my memory.

And maybe, like me, you've carried your own silent memories, trying to make sense of what you saw.

If so, I want you to know you're not alone.

God saw me on that radiator and covered me, even in unsafe places.

I know He sees you too.

Truth Be Told

*Truth be told, in places like dope houses, where kids don't belong, **first come, first served** wasn't just a phrase. It was my reality inside my mother's addiction. It was how people showed up at the door, ready to be served something that was poisoning their bodies, their families, and their children, not just in that moment but for years afterwards.*

But what I've come to understand is this. My spirit was never meant to wait in line behind pain, behind fear, or behind my mother's choices.

My healing, my truth, and my peace come first now.

Writing to help others is my way of serving God's people. I've learned to put myself first fully, knowing that God will use me to serve others from a place of wholeness, not brokenness.

LET'S DO THE HEART WORK

Take your time here. This is your space to release what you've seen, what you've held in silence, and what you've never told anyone. Write as you are. God can handle your honesty, your grief, and your questions.

The Heart Work For

Adult Children of Addicts

What is a memory you've carried in silence?

- What happened, and where were you?
- What do you remember seeing, hearing, or feeling?
- What did you tell yourself in that moment to keep going?
- What have you never said out loud about that memory?

What did it feel like to witness addiction as a child or teen?

- How did it feel in your body to see your parent in that state?
- What emotions did you have to hide to keep yourself safe?
- How did you learn to watch and wait, and what did it cost you?
- Who did you become in order to survive?

If someone had asked you back then, "Are you okay?" what would you have said?

- What would you have wanted them to ask instead?
- What would you have needed to feel safe enough to tell the truth?
- If you could speak to your younger self in that moment, what would you say now?

The Heart Work for Parents in Recovery

What do you remember about the moments your child saw you using or struggling?

- What was happening in your life during that season?
- How did you feel when you saw your child watching?
- What do you wish you could say to your child about those moments now?

What would it mean to start seeing yourself with kindness as you heal?

- How have you seen yourself in the past, and what parts of that story are you ready to let go?
- What would it look like to see yourself the way God sees you?
- What does restoration, within yourself and with your child mean to you now?
- How has your relationship with your child shifted because of your healing, and where do you still hope to grow?

What does healing look like for you now?

- What does recovery mean to you beyond sobriety?
- Who do you want to or who have you become as you heal?
- What does a "safe space" look like for you now, and how can you create it?
- What would you write in a letter to your child about your healing?

Breath Break Before You Continue

Before moving into your next chapter or reflection, take a **Breath Break** to honor your body and spirit:

- Sit comfortably and place one hand on your heart, one hand on your belly.
- Inhale deeply through your nose for a count of 4, hold for a count of 4, and exhale slowly through your mouth for a count of 6.
- As you breathe, say quietly to yourself: *"I am safe. I am allowed to rest. I am allowed to heal."*
- Repeat this breathing cycle three times, letting your shoulders drop with each exhale.
- Allow yourself to notice any tension you are holding and give yourself permission to release it.

When you are ready, thank yourself for showing up to your heart work, and continue your journey at your own gentle pace.

CHAPTER THREE: Save For A Rainy Day

The innocent courage to cry and a
Grandmother who listened.

People say save money for a rainy day. But after a few trips to the dope house with my mom, I learned it wasn't money that would save me.

It was Granny and something I innocently said one day.

Before I tell you how Granny saved me, I can't help but reflect on all the good times we shared and all the good her house gave me.

Granny was the glue that held our family together. She saved me in ways I don't even think my family knows. She gave my childhood balance. Her house on seventy-sixth and King Drive, that oversized four-bedroom Georgian brick on the South Side, was more than a house. It was a safe place. A place where everyone stayed when they fell on hard times. A place to breathe, laugh, and belong in the middle of all the chaos that came with being a dope fiend's daughter.

Granny's house sat proud on the block, right next to an eight-unit building. Early on, it was dark brick, but Papa had it sandblasted, turning it into a reddish brick with white mortar that caught the sun just right. Granny kept the lawn cut clean, edges sharp, and after years of driving down King Drive to Mission of Faith Baptist Church admiring other folks' red trees, she finally planted her own. She painted the tree trunk white and wrote "Beasley" and our address on it, like she was staking a claim that we were here, no matter what.

We'd sit on the big white wooden porch on iron furniture bolted down, flapping the mail slot to get in since there was no doorbell. I can still hear that clanking echoing through the house with its popcorn ceilings and mirrored walls, reflecting the light and making the space feel bigger than it was.

The décor made people think we were rich, but it didn't show the candles we lit when the lights were out, the jugs we filled when the water was cut off, or the pots we boiled to take baths when the gas was off.

Inside, marble floors kissed our feet, and the plush white carpet on the stairs had a clear plastic runner we'd better not step off. On the landing, a large fish tank bubbled quietly, glowing with orange and yellow fish. I'd pause to watch them before bed, listening to the sound of water like a soft lullaby.

To the right of the house, when stepping into the living and dining rooms, we'd sometimes be greeted by upside-down plastic runners that bit at our feet with sharp spikes. That was Granny's way of keeping her carpet and sacred areas clean. The Rossi Brothers white living room furniture, wrapped in protective plastic covers, would stick to our legs in the summer, squeaking every time we tried to peel ourselves off.

The dining room's china cabinet stayed locked with dishes we could see but never touch. The eight-seat table was always set with gold-rimmed plates and utensils, ready for company whether they came or not. The fifty-gallon fish tank full of exotic fish and bottom-feeding catfish gave the room a soft evening glow. There were golden gates that marked the entry to the dining room, a fancy touch from Granny, even though we usually crawled under them anyway.

The den sat at the back of the house, right off the kitchen. Its plush pink carpet, white wicker furniture, and black-floral cushions was where Granny watched Wheel of Fortune while she cooked and where we all gathered when we came together. Her presence filled the room, even if she didn't say a word.

And then there was the kitchen. The smell of bleach, Murphy's oil soap, and home-cooked food lived there. That's where Granny worked her magic, sometimes from scratch, sometimes flipping food she brought home from Saint Joseph Hospital into feasts.

Granny loved to visit the field to pick greens and vegetables. She'd bring home garbage bags of collard, mustard, and turnip greens.

Her greens were seasoned just right, hot water cornbread crumbled perfectly, and duck dressing had the perfect color and spices. We didn't like that light-skinned dressing. Her seafood gumbo was packed with flavor—lobster tails, shrimp, chicken, and Parker House hot links. Her shrimp and crab salad had just the right kick, and her signature peach cobbler made our mouths water the moment we saw the ingredients laid out.

Right before the back door, the cabinet to the left held glass mason jars of chow-chow for our greens and peach preserves she spread on hot biscuits and toast.

Out back, the deck Papa built in the 90s overflowed with Granny's pink potted flowers every summer. We had cookouts, family gatherings, even weddings out there. King, our German Shepherd, lived under the porch in the 80s. He barked at the world, ate our leftovers, never saw a leash or a vet, but he was part of the family.

Granny had caramel skin and curves women pay to have, and she moved through the house and anywhere else she went with unmatched confidence. One day she'd be sweeping in a floral nightgown, humming. The next, she'd be stepping out in a leopard catsuit or sequined dress, her heels clicking across the marble like she owned the world.

She might smile at you, cuss you out, help you with something, and then quietly stir a pot of beans like nothing happened.

We called it Granny's house, but Papa lived there too. He wasn't around as much. He ran lounges and worked as an interior decorator, but his touch was in the house, the open walls between rooms, the mirrors, the layout. Still, it was Granny's warmth that made it home.

Because of my mom's instability, we often lived with Granny. It was the safest place for me.

Not every day at Granny's was easy. The morning arguments were sometimes my alarm clock. Between Granny and Papa, or sometimes with my mom about missing money or jewelry she'd sold for a high. I didn't understand all the fighting, but I knew once it was over, Granny would bring peace back into the house with a meal or her beautiful smile.

Some of my best memories at the house were with my cousins. There were seven of us, and we were thick as thieves. Sleepovers meant "snickling all night," as Granny would say. We played hide-and-seek, Rock Teacher on the front steps, Double Dutch, hopscotch with rocks, red light-green light in the yard, and hand games like "twee lee-lee."

We stuffed ourselves with sour pickles and peppermint sticks, penny candy, Hot Stuff chips, Doritos with hot sauce. We soaked sunflower seeds in vinegar and spit them all over Granny's porch while she fussed about them damn pumpkin seeds. We warmed up the chocolate chip cookies she brought from St. Joseph's, and they tasted like safety in a world that often wasn't.

We even named the rooms. The sewing room, The Big Room, and the Blue Room. The Big Room was where we'd often sleep. My cousin and I, closest in age, would always jump in the bouncy bed in the Big Room and make up silly songs we still remember to this day.

The tiny half-bathroom on the first floor was the only entry to the basement. If someone was on the toilet downstairs, they had to brace their feet against the basement entry so no one came in. Which meant that if you were in the basement and someone was on the toilet, you were stuck down there until they finished. That's just how it worked. The door didn't lock. It was awkward, but we figured it out.

We spent time in the basement as well. Running around, listening to music, watching TV, and some of us would sneak sips from Papa's liquor stash. We drank so much of some of the bottles of vodka, gin, and Peppermint Schnapps that we filled the bottles with water when they got too low. Granny, Papa, or none of my aunts or uncles ever checked to see if we'd been sneaking sips.

My cousins and I laughed, fought, made up, and started all over again. But even in the joy, my mom's addiction showed up in jokes and side comments. My cousins really didn't respect her. One called her a bitch and ran. I remember how she chased him in her black robe from room to room and whooped him good when he was caught. Another cousin squeezed out all my mom's nasal spray and replaced it with bleach.

When he did that, I laughed to fit in, but I couldn't stay quiet about that. I told my mom. Because even if I was mad at her for her addiction, I still wanted her safe.

Granny's house was like my life. Joy wrapped around hidden trauma. Like the time, around age four or five, when my mom had just fried some potatoes she'd cut up for us. She always poured the hot grease over the back porch. One winter night she went to dump the grease and slipped on ice. She screamed so loud I froze.

I didn't cry. When she managed to get back in, I helped her. I peeled off her shoes and pants, each pull taking a piece of her skin with it. And in all my innocence, I said, "Momma, your leg was frying like some chicken." I don't know if she laughed, but I smile when I think about it now.

She got to the hospital and got bandaged up. At home, taking care of those burns was tedious, but that still didn't keep her from going out to get high.

I loved both my parents. Most of the time, if Granny told me to go with my mom, I wanted to. I wanted to believe she would take care of me, that she was better this time, that maybe things would be different.

But deep down, even as a little girl, I was learning how to tell when something wasn't right.

And one rainy day, I found the courage to innocently say it out loud.

I was around six. The rain tapped the windows. The mail slot clanked in the wind as my mom grabbed my hand to leave. My feet wouldn't move. Tears ran down my chubby cheeks.

Granny came down the stairs, not ready for what I was about to say.

"LaTanya, what's wrong?"

"I don't want to go."

"Why?"

"Because they always be putting that stuff in they nose."

That was all I had to say.

Granny gave my mom a side-eyed look, then took my hand and led me back upstairs.

From that day on, I stayed.

She never made me leave with my mom again. She took care of me. And over time, people didn't understand why she did more for my brother and me than for the other grandkids. One day, in a heated moment, she told them the truth. She did more because we didn't have the same chances; because of my mother's addiction, we didn't have the stability or support the other grandkids had.

My family didn't know about that rainy day. But I did. Granny did.

That's why I was always there.

Looking back now, I see how much Granny's house wasn't just a house. It was a lifeline. I didn't know it then, but every laugh with my cousins, every squeak of that plastic-covered couch, every bite of Granny's food was stitching survival into me.

It's wild how a kid can hold fear and joy in the same breath. How you can love your parents deeply and still be scared of what they're doing to themselves.

That rainy day, when I said I didn't want to go, was the day I chose something different for myself, even if I didn't know it yet.

Granny gave me that choice. And I am forever grateful.

Some moments change everything.

That rainy day was mine.

Granny saved me.

Truth Be Told

Truth be told. What does it really mean to "save for a rainy day"? For me, it was never about money. It was about memories, people, and those small sacred moments when love showed up right on time.

Granny's house wasn't just bricks and furniture. It was a shelter for my spirit. A place that reminded me who I was, even when my circumstances tried to pull me into something darker.

Looking back now, I understand. Granny wasn't saving money for me. She was saving me. In her quiet, stubborn way, she was storing up laughter, warmth, home-cooked meals, and discipline. It was like a savings account of love I could draw from whenever life turned cold and gray.

That rainy day, when I cried out in innocence and she took my hand, wasn't just the day she saved me from visiting a place I didn't belong. It was the day she showed me I had a choice. A choice to speak up, ask for help, and say no to chaos. A choice to believe there was someone who saw me and wanted to protect me.

Years later, I realize I've been living off the interest of what Granny saved for me ever since that rainy day.

LET'S DO THE HEART WORK

Take your time here. Let your heart speak freely with no edits, no fear, no judgment. Breathe. Pray. Let God meet you as you write.

The Heart Work
For Adult Children Of Addicts

Who was your "safe person" growing up?

- What did they do that made you feel safe?
- How did you feel when you were around them?
- What did you wish you could have told them about what was happening in your life?
- Are there ways you can honor the safety they gave you now as an adult?

What was your "safe place" as a child or teen?

- Where did you feel the most peace or protection?
- What details do you remember about that place (smells, sounds, colors)?
- How did that place help you survive what you couldn't control?
- How can you create a version of that safe place for yourself today?

Have you ever spoken up about something that hurt you?

- What did it feel like to say the truth out loud?
- Who did you tell, and what happened after you shared it?
- What truths are you still holding inside?
- What would it mean to let those truths be spoken now?

The Heart Work for Parents in Recovery

What does being a "safe place" for your child mean to you?

- Who was a safe person for you when you were younger?
- What did you learn about safety (or the lack of it) growing up?
- How can you begin to create safety for your child now, even if it wasn't always there before?

What does it look like to let God help you heal your family story?

- What fears do you have about being honest with your child about your past?
- What hopes do you have for your relationship with them?
- What does forgiveness (from God, from your child, and toward yourself) look like to you?

Breath Break Before You Continue

Before moving into your next chapter or reflection, take a
Breath Break to honor your body and spirit:

- Sit comfortably and place one hand on your heart, one hand on your belly.
- Inhale deeply through your nose for a count of 4, hold for a count of 4, and exhale slowly through your mouth for a count of 6.
- As you breathe, say quietly to yourself: *"I am safe. I am allowed to rest. I am allowed to heal."*
- Repeat this breathing cycle three times, letting your shoulders drop with each exhale.
- Allow yourself to notice any tension you are holding and give yourself permission to release it.

When you are ready, thank yourself for showing up to your
heart work, and continue your journey at your own gentle pace.

CHAPTER FOUR: My Brother's Keeper

A reflection on how love, responsibility, and childhood survival shaped the bond between a sister and her brother.

At sixteen, I wrote the poem that landed me in therapy.

What I didn't know then was that nineteen years earlier, when my mother was just fifteen, she got introduced to heroin. Not by a dealer, not by her boyfriend. By her own brother.

He didn't do it to hurt her. He loved her. He wasn't trying to ruin her life, he just brought her into his world. That's how it starts sometimes. You think you're just sharing something, not realizing what you're really passing on.

Nobody thought about how something you try for fun can turn into years of pain, or how it can mess up a whole family. Nobody meant for that to happen. But that's where it started.

Back then, pain felt normal. Or euphoric. She was handed poison and called it relief. When she should've been in high school with friends, talking about dances and dreams and the future, she was already chasing a high.

I was born when she was twenty-one. For years, I never wanted to know whether I had heroin in my system at birth. I never had the courage to ask.

In families like mine, some things get told right away. Other things just hang in the air until you finally decide to ask. Some answers you're given, some you have to go looking for.

In 2021, I found out the truth.

Not through a conversation, not through one of those heart-to-hearts people say mothers and daughters are supposed to have.

I found out because I read it in a book she co-authored, *Raising Daughters*.

She wrote about her addiction. How it started at fifteen. How her brother introduced her to heroin. How the years that followed broke her down. But in the middle of her story, almost like a side note, was the part I had been wondering about for years.

When she found out she was pregnant with me, she told her doctor about her addiction. That's how she got connected to the methadone program.

She cared enough to try. She didn't want DCFS involved when I was born. Kids who grew up around addiction know what that means. She wanted me to have a fighting chance.

I wasn't born with heroin in my system. I was born withdrawing from methadone.

It's a different fight, but still a fight.

I came into this world uncomfortable, crying, shaking, my body reacting to something it didn't ask for.

Reading those pages helped me understand my beginning. It didn't erase what came after, it didn't soften the memories or change the fact that I had to grow up fast. But it gave me something I didn't have before. Clarity.

My brother's story wasn't the same. When he was born, it wasn't methadone. It was heroin.

May 28, 1986.

The day my brother John was born.

He was beautiful, jet-black hair slicked down, slanted little eyes like a Chinese baby. Behind all that softness, he was crying, shaking, already fighting to live without a drug he didn't ask for.

I remember the hospital. Too bright, machines humming, that antiseptic smell stuck to everything, including my clothes.

There was a thick glass barrier between us, like the one at Cook County Jail when I visited my mother. A wall that keeps you from touching the people you love.

John wasn't shaking as much anymore, but he cried like his heart was breaking. Even as a kid, I felt his pain. I'd heard whispers from adults, so I knew exactly what it was.

Once he finally detoxed and was healthy enough, John came home.

At first, he was sweet, respectful, cute as could be.

But by three or four, he lived up to his nickname: Bad Ass.

He cursed, talked back. One time, he squirted dish soap in Granny's fish tank and all the fish died. Granny was heartbroken.

John just shrugged and said, "Well, the fish ate all the bubbles."

I shouldn't have laughed, but I did. I still do.

He was loud, wild, fearless. My aunt gave him that name, John "Bad Ass," and it stuck until he grew out of it around six or seven.

Somewhere along the way, he became my responsibility. No conversation, no paperwork. One day, my mother just stopped walking him to and from school.

And suddenly, getting him there and taking care of him afterward fell on me.

It didn't matter that I was just a kid myself.

I was in sixth grade, cheerleading, dancing, trying to do normal girl stuff. But I couldn't go anywhere without asking:

"Can my little brother come with me?"
"Is it okay if he sits in the back while I practice?"

Sometimes people said yes. Other times, "Go find a babysitter," like I was somebody's mama.

I wasn't. But I was carrying it like I was.

That weight turned into resentment. That resentment turned into anger. And that anger turned into abuse.

I didn't have the words to explain how mad I was, so I took it out on him.

I punched him in the back. I picked fights for no reason.

One time, I beat him so bad he had purple bruises running up and down his spine.

My mother saw them.

"What happened to you?"

John looked her in the eyes and said, "I fell."

She showed somebody else. He stuck with the same story.

He protected me, even after what I did.

I felt horrible then and I still feel horrible now.

Most of that happened while we still lived with Granny. Back when I was juggling school and cheerleading and trying to act like I had a normal life, all while taking care of my little brother like he was my responsibility. That's where a lot of my anger came out. In that house. On him.

Eventually, we moved out of Granny's house into a basement apartment a few doors down. Roach-infested, roaches so bold they hung out on the porch in broad daylight like they lived there too.

At night, I pictured them crawling everywhere; behind the stove, under the fridge, scaling the walls while I tried to sleep.

My skin would itch for no reason. I'd slap at my arms, I was sure something was crawling on me, even when it wasn't.

Even now, thinking about those nights makes my skin crawl. Some things leave when you move out, but roaches and that feeling? They stay with you.

One day I had friends over. John followed me around like always. I got so fed up about having to watch him again, I started kicking him. Didn't care who saw.

But that day, John was tired too.

He picked up a piece of his thick black plastic race car track, the kind you had to snap together to make those little loops.

Without saying a word, he whacked me across my back like he was done.

And honestly, that moment made me done too.

He didn't cry, he didn't run, he just looked at me like, try it again if you want to.

And you know what?
I never laid hands on him again.
Something changed in both of us that day.

John grew out of his "Bad Ass" phase.

He became kind, respectful, the kind of person who lights up a room without trying.

People love John.

And if you don't like John, it probably says more about you than it does about him.

I understand him now.

He helps me and I help him.

And even after everything, I wouldn't change having been responsible for him. I still look out for him when I can. He does the same for me.

Even with all of that, there were little moments where people showed up for me, moments that reminded me I was still a kid, even if I didn't always get to feel like one.

Like the time I got invited to a sleepover at Danielle's house.

She always threw the best ones. I was excited. It felt like maybe, just for one night, I could be a regular kid.

But my mother had other plans.

She told me I couldn't go unless I took John with me.

She was home... not working, not out.

She was in her room, getting high, the smell of curling irons and that stinky Primo spray from Walgreens in the air whenever she opened the door. She never unplugged those curlers; they stayed hot for hours, sometimes days. I knew better than to touch them, but that didn't mean I never stepped on them.

Instead of doing what a mother is supposed to do, she handed it off to me.

I was furious. I was embarrassed. But I asked anyway.

My heart was pounding like I was asking for something I didn't cause.

My mother didn't even call my friend's mom herself, even though they knew each other from Ruggles. Graduated the same year. Family knew family.

Why did she make me, a twelve-year-old girl, make that call?

I swallowed my pride and called.

I told her I wanted to come, but my mother said I couldn't go unless I brought John with me.

She didn't shame me, she didn't ask questions.

"He can come, Tanya. It's fine. He can play with my son."

That night, Danielle's mom let me be a kid.

She took care of John. She didn't put it back on me.

She gave me a little piece of childhood when I needed it most.

To this day, that story still brings tears to my eyes. That's why I love and appreciate her. Not just for what she did, but for the kind of person she showed me she was. She gave me a small break when she didn't even know how much I needed one.

But I knew.

Sometimes when I think about family, about what we give each other and what we take from each other, I come back to that difference. My mother's brother handed her heroin. One sibling gave another something that changed everything.

And I think about John.

No matter how mad I was, I would never hand him something that could hurt him.

I was angry. I was abusive. But I love my brother.

I'm still his keeper.

And he never stopped being mine.

Writing this brought up things I kept buried for years.

I told my husband and my friends about how mean I was, how John finally whacked me with that racetrack. We laughed about it.

But I never told John. I never had that conversation with him.

I didn't know if he remembered, if he resented me.

Honestly, it's embarrassing to admit. I wanted to bury it like we bury so many family secrets.

But I didn't.

A few days before writing this, I called John. I asked what he remembered about growing up, hanging out with me and my friends.

He talked about the good times, riding the bus to Jackson Park, playing alone at the field house while I danced.

Back then, we didn't know how dangerous that could've been. A little boy alone with no food, no water, no supervision. Looking back now, I see it.

He talked about funny TV shows we watched, the small stuff that clearly meant something to him.

I inhaled. I hesitated.

"Do you remember how mean I was? How abusive I was to you?"

He said no.

He didn't remember the bruises, the screaming, the racetrack.

He vaguely remembered the sleepover, playing with my friend's brother.

John remembered the good times with his big sister.

While I carried guilt, he carried joy.

That took a huge weight off my conscience.

It showed me how important it is to face what haunts us, to let go of the stuff we carry in silence. Especially when it comes to the people we love.

I'm glad I asked him.

Whether he remembers or not, I feel free.

I don't look back in guilt anymore.

We made it, through the yelling, the bruises, the roaches, the bus stops, through the days I cared and the days I didn't, through the weight of a past trying to stick to us.

I was born into her addiction. He was born fighting something he didn't ask for.

But we're here.

Drug-free. Still holding each other up.

Truth Be Told

"Am I my brother's keeper?" They said it in New Jack City, *and that line stuck with a lot of us who grew up in the '90s. But the truth is, it started long before that.*

Being my brother's keeper meant carrying him when I was still learning to walk through life myself. It meant watching over him while wishing someone would watch over me. It meant protecting him from the world while trying to survive it too.

Looking back, I see that in all the ways I tried to keep him, he kept me too. His laughter, his forgiveness, his quiet loyalty was a soft place for me to land in a life that was sometimes hard.

Instead of looking back in guilt, I look at John now and see that we made it. We made it through the heaviness of a past that tried to stick to us. And even though I was born into her addiction, and he was born fighting something he didn't ask for, we're here.

Drug-free. And we lived to see our mother's sobriety. She lived to see our forgiveness.

If you're reading this, I hope you know that being someone's keeper doesn't mean you have to lose yourself. It means learning that love can be heavy and healing at the same time, and that you deserve to be kept too.

LET'S DO THE HEART WORK:
My Brother's Keeper

Take your time here. Breathe. Let your heart speak what it needs to say, even if it's messy. God can handle your honesty and so can these pages.

The Heart Work For Adult Children Of Addicts

Who did you feel responsible for when you were growing up?

- Who were you forced to care for before you were ready?
- How did that responsibility feel in your body and mind?
- What did you lose in yourself while trying to protect someone else?
- What parts of you grew stronger because of it?

Did you ever resent the people you had to protect?

- What did you wish you could say to them at the time?
- What feelings did you hide under anger or frustration?
- How did you handle guilt or shame around your resentment?
- What would it feel like to release that hidden truth now?

What memories have you carried that you need to revisit?

- What is one memory you've been afraid to talk about?
- What does it feel like to bring it into the light here?
- What would it mean to forgive yourself for how you coped?
- How has God shown you grace in hidden places of your story?

The Heart Work for Parents in Recovery

Have your children supported you in ways children shouldn't have to?

- What are some moments that come to mind?
- How do you think your child felt in those times?
- How have you seen your child's strengths through those experiences?
- How can you honor the ways your family has grown together?

What would you like your child to know about your story?

- What would you share with them if you could write them a letter?
- How would you want them to see you today?
- What hopes do you have for your relationship now?
- How can you create space for your child to share their story with you too?

Breath Break Before You Continue

Before moving into your next chapter or reflection, take a **Breath Break** to honor your body and spirit:

- Sit comfortably and place one hand on your heart, one hand on your belly.
- Inhale deeply through your nose for a count of 4, hold for a count of 4, and exhale slowly through your mouth for a count of 6.
- As you breathe, say quietly to yourself: *"I am safe. I am allowed to rest. I am allowed to heal."*
- Repeat this breathing cycle three times, letting your shoulders drop with each exhale.
- Allow yourself to notice any tension you are holding and give yourself permission to release it.

When you are ready, thank yourself for showing up to your heart work, and continue your journey at your own gentle pace.

*"In every relationship, healing begins when
blame ends and understanding begins."*
Unknown

CHAPTER FIVE:
A Penny For Your Thoughts

The story of how 500 pennies went from a hopeful moment into full blown rage.

In our basement apartment inside a roach-infested house, we did our best to keep our space clean. When I was around eleven, we'd moved two houses down from Granny's place into the basement of a gray-and-white stone house on seventy-sixth and King Drive.

Granny's protection had shifted by then. She went from saving me from my mother's mess to being more of a financial support system. Most of my mom's public aid check went toward rent.

Our entrance was on the side of the house. We had an ugly green chipped wooden door and a screen door with no glass, the kind that swung open and slammed shut if you even looked at it wrong. You had to walk down about five steps to reach the "plush" royal blue carpet. It was rough, worn, but still better than our neighbor's place.

Dark brown wood paneling covered every wall, holding on to the smell of incense and Primo, that cheap Walgreens spray my mother used, the scent working overtime to cover up not just our space, but whatever was drifting in from next door.

We had a cloth, cream-colored floral couch and loveseat set, and a coffee table that left just enough room for my friends and me to choreograph whatever new routine we planned to debut at The Rink that weekend. Sometimes we practiced inside, sometimes on the porch, sometimes on the sidewalk. Wherever there was rhythm, we made room for release.

After becoming involuntarily partially responsible for my brother while still trying to hold on to whatever fun I could grab as a kid, The Rink Fitness Factory on Saturday nights was my lifeline. The Rink was my relief and my escape, and I grew more popular with every visit.

While The Rink was the place to be on Saturday nights in the '90s, nobody really went there to skate. I lived on the small practice floor, shoulder to shoulder with other kids who had something to prove, something to forget, or in my case, both.

I danced until my fan ponytail gave out, my brown gel stopped holding, and my outfit was soaked in the sweat of a girl who released it all after holding it all in, week after week.

Getting to The Rink was never easy. My mother barely had five dollars to spare. Sometimes I'd beg. Sometimes I'd borrow. A lot of times, my friend's mom would give me money to get in and give us a ride there and back. Most times, I robbed a piggy bank or two.

One Saturday, my friend and I had everything lined up. We'd practiced our dance all week. We had matching outfits. My friend had money. We even had a ride. I had collected 500 pennies. I was ready to go.

My plan was to walk to the Currency Exchange on 75th and Calumet and trade them in for a five-dollar bill. I'd been getting ready since that morning, because back then, we wore our same all-day outfits straight to The Rink.

I was dressed, cheap body spray layered over the sweat of dancing earlier, coins heavy in my pocket, heart pounding with excitement. I was out the door.

And then… my mother.

She stepped out of her room, the stale smell of incense and that Walgreens spray drifting out as the door creaked. Her eyes low, coming down from a high or getting ready for her next one, and suddenly, she decided to be a parent.

"Where you going?"

"To The Rink."

"You're not going this week."

"Why?"

"Because I said so."

That was it. No reason. No explanation. Just her, deciding at the last minute to play mother.

She hadn't checked on me all week. Hadn't asked if I ate, if I was okay, or if I needed anything. But now, suddenly, she wanted to tell me where I couldn't go. Like I hadn't earned it. Like I didn't deserve this one small thing I looked forward to.

In my mind, all she ever said to me was, "You need to take John with you," but now she wanted to speak on what I couldn't do. I asked again. She gave me the same answer, flat and final, like I didn't even deserve a reason.

That's when it happened.

My pulse roared in my ears, heat rising in my chest and my neck, the weight of those pennies pressing into my palm like they were daring me to let go. And I did.

Before I knew it, I was yelling, "I'm sick of you!" and those 500 pennies went flying across the living room, hitting her, hitting the couch, hitting the table, bouncing off the wall, clinking against that old wood paneling, filling the room with the sound of my breaking point.

My friend couldn't believe what I had done. She didn't say a word, but her eyes showed me how surprised she was by my actions.

My mom told my friend to leave. The screen door slammed, rattling the frame, like it always did, and then it was just me and her.

I threw all the pillows off the couch. I slammed my hands against the walls, the wood paneling shaking under each hit.

I stomped, kicked, screamed, the air hot in my throat, my breathing heavy and ragged. I raged like I needed a white jacket with straps.

I saw it in her eyes that night; fear.

I'm sure she was wondering, what in the hell is going on with this girl.

All the years of holding it in, watching her disappear into that room, being home but unavailable for me and John, getting high behind that door, letting strangers walk in and out of our lives, that night, it all came out.

I told her everything.

I told her I was tired of being her babysitter. Tired of cut-up straws with powdery residue being left around the house. Tired of watching John. Tired of making her be the parent and demanding part of that public aid check. Tired of stepping on her hot curling irons she never cut off. Tired of being the oldest, the responsible one, the forgotten one. Tired of being the one who carried what she refused to claim.

And you know what? That night... I was heard. She listened to me and I didn't get in trouble for my actions.

When it was over, the room was a mess. So was I.

My chest was tight, my eyes were red and swollen from crying, my hands shaking, and I had a metallic taste in my mouth from screaming so hard. I remember looking around at the pennies scattered across the floor, the couch, the table, like tiny reminders of everything I carried and released.

Ironically, I remember the song, *One Last Cry* by Brian McKnight playing on the radio in the calm after my storm. It wasn't my last cry. I was still living in addiction, but something about the song was touching in that moment.

Today, the song is still a reminder of my first out of control episode.

I didn't feel free, but I felt lighter for the first time. Not because I didn't have those pennies in my pocket anymore, but because I had said what I needed to say, even if it came out in screams.

Nothing changed with her. But for me, it was the start of many of my rages.

It was also the moment something changed in my eyes when I looked in the mirror. Eyes swollen and red, face still wet, there was a hardness that hadn't been there before. A promise to myself that I would keep speaking up, even if it wasn't pretty.

Truth Be Told

They say, "A penny for your thoughts," meaning your thoughts and feelings are worth hearing and matter, even if it feels like no one has valued them before.

But for me, it was 500 pennies that finally let my thoughts be heard.

I didn't know that rage could be a language when silence was all I knew. I didn't know that throwing those pennies would crack something open in me, creating a small space where my voice could finally exist.

I was the daughter of not one, but two dope fiends. And I've learned that sometimes it takes a storm of scattered pennies to prove that my thoughts, my anger, my truth, and my voice are worth more than anyone ever told me.

If you're reading this, let me offer you a penny for your thoughts; and remind you that speaking them out loud, or writing them down, might just set you free.

LET'S DO THE HEART WORK:

A Penny For Your Thoughts

You deserve the space to process these parts of your story gently, at your own pace. Let these questions guide you with compassion as you continue your healing and reclaim your voice, piece by piece.

The Heart Work
For Adult Children Of Addicts

What brought you joy when everything around you felt heavy?

- Where did you go to feel like yourself?
- What moments made you feel free, even if only for a little while?
- Who or what made you smile when life felt unfair?

Have you ever held in your feelings until they exploded?
- What were you holding in, and why?
- What did it feel like in your body before you finally spoke up?
- What did you wish you could say that you didn't?
- What would it feel like to let yourself speak your truth safely now?

What responsibilities did you carry that weren't yours to hold?

- Who or what were you protecting?
- How did you feel carrying that weight?
- How did you find moments to still be a kid, even in small ways?
- How can you acknowledge your strength without having to keep carrying that weight today?

The Heart Work for Parents in Recovery

Have you ever seen your child express anger or pain in ways that surprised you?
- What happened in that moment?
- How did you feel seeing your child's hurt come out in anger?
- What do you think your child was trying to say through that moment?
- How can you hold space for your child's feelings today, even if it's hard to hear?

What would you want your child to know now about your heart?

- What would you say to your child if you could talk about that moment today?
- How have you seen your child's strength through their feelings?
- What do you want your child to know about who you are becoming now?
- What does it look like to grow and heal together, one conversation at a time?

BREATH BREAK BEFORE YOU CONTINUE

Before moving into your next chapter or reflection, take a **Breath Break** to honor your body and spirit:

- Sit comfortably and place one hand on your heart, one hand on your belly.
- Inhale deeply through your nose for a count of 4, hold for a count of 4, and exhale slowly through your mouth for a count of 6.
- As you breathe, say quietly to yourself: *"I am safe. I am allowed to rest. I am allowed to heal."*
- Repeat this breathing cycle three times, letting your shoulders drop with each exhale.
- Allow yourself to notice any tension you are holding and give yourself permission to release it.

When you are ready, thank yourself for showing up to your heart work, and continue your journey at your own gentle pace.

"Your story could be the key that unlocks someone else's prison. Speak up."
— Unknown

CHAPTER SIX: It's Not Rocket Science

Teased. Labeled. Humiliated.
Until I snapped, right there in science class.

Stability was a stranger to me in the earlier part of my life. We moved constantly, which meant I changed schools and friends just as often.

I started kindergarten at Martha Ruggles Elementary on the South Side of Chicago. I made it halfway through first grade there, right around the time my mother married John's father, Michael, in Granny's house.

Not long after, we moved to Hammond, Indiana, closer than most Chicago suburbs, but with a state line in between. I finished both first and second grade at Caldwell Elementary.

I remember coming home from a friend's house one day and seeing all of our things outside. My clothes, my toys, everything out in the open for the world to see. My mother and Michael were standing outside with it all. I asked why, and my mother told me we were moving back to Granny's house for a little while. The way our belongings were just tossed out like that felt strange, but later, I realized we'd been evicted.

A few weeks after we moved in with Granny, we were back in Chicago and moving again. This time, we moved to a subsidized apartment on 68th and Perry. A few months after that move, I started third grade at Yale Elementary, but I only stayed for a quarter.

Just as I was settling in, meeting new friends, it was time to pack up again.

Next stop: Mobile, Alabama. Third grade at Forest Hill Elementary.

Why the move? I guess they thought a new environment might help them get clean. But addicts don't leave addiction behind. They just pack it up and bring it with them. Without rehab, they were still using. The location changed. The addiction didn't.

That summer after third grade, I was sent back to Chicago to stay with family and ended up at my aunt's house in Bellwood. She worked nights at the post office, slept through the days, and wasn't exactly hovering. When my mom called with my return flight details to Alabama, I didn't tell my aunt. Not once.

How irresponsible of both of them, right?

I missed every single flight on purpose.

By the time school started in the fall, I was still in Bellwood. My mom gave up on Alabama altogether. I don't know exactly what happened between her and Michael, but whatever it was, she packed up, rented a U-Haul, and hauled ass back to Chicago without him, but with John.

When she pulled up to my aunt's house in the U-Haul she'd driven from Mobile, school had already been in session for weeks. My mother had decided to stay in Bellwood with my aunt for a while.

I enrolled late, three weeks into fourth grade, at Roosevelt Elementary.

And that's when it started. My first real taste of bullying.

One day at recess, I was running, laughing, the slap of my shoes echoing against the cement. The wind stuck my bangs to my forehead. Then bam, I was face-first sliding across the pavement like I was trying to reach third base.

That hot concrete scraped and burned my skin. Gravel bit into my cheek. Blood and dirt filled my mouth. The air smelled like tar. Kids yelled, but it sounded far away, like I was underwater. Everything was black, a blur.

What did I do? What just happened? Why me? I remember thinking as I pushed myself up, palms burning.

All the teachers rushed to me, calling for paper towels and napkins to catch the blood running down my face. Their reaction scared me. Made me cry. The tears burned like hot coals against my scraped skin.

Then I realized what happened.

Some little nappy-headed boy pushed me for no reason. I figured he learned somewhere it was okay to hurt girls. He never apologized.

He became the ringleader of something worse. After the swelling went down and the big ugly bandages were no longer needed, the scar marked my face in an ugly way. He teased me about it calling me "Spud," like Spuds MacKenzie, that beer-commercial dog from the '80s.

It stuck.

Not just from him. All the boys in class called me that for the rest of fourth grade.

Spud.

I wasn't the prettiest. I wasn't the most put-together. But I didn't look like no damn dog.

I still remember my fourth-grade school photo. My face was half-healed, still scarred. I forced a smile because I didn't see myself as pretty behind that scar.

The interesting thing about that photo is that before the fall, I had already taken my school pictures. My hair was nicely done, a bang, a middle ponytail, and the back was down. I'd slept in those uncomfortable pink sponge rollers the night before to make sure my hair was nice and curly.

My mother paid for my photos late, and somehow the wires got crossed. The school thought she'd requested a retake. I told them she hadn't. I told them that I wanted to keep the cute photos I'd already seen, the ones where I wore a nice dress and my hair was done pretty. But I was just a fourth-grader, standing there in a yellow sweater I wore twice a week, with an ugly scar on my face. Of course, they didn't listen. Instead, they insisted I take a new photo.

In life, everything happens for a reason. That fourth-grade photo I ended up with has become the focal point of so many stories, including this one.

Over time my face healed, I met and hung out with new friends, but as usual, that summer it was time to go. We moved again. Me, my mom, my aunt, and cousins moved to Maywood, on 19th Avenue. We were only there briefly. Just long enough for some landlord drama and foreclosure to push us right back to Granny's house.

By the time we figured out we were staying at Granny's for a while, school had already started again. I still hadn't enrolled, so there I was, starting fifth grade late again. But at least I was back at

Ruggles, home of the Rockets, a school where my aunts, uncles, and cousins had attended and graduated.

Believe it or not, I finally had some stability.

I stayed there through eighth grade. But stability didn't mean peace.

By seventh grade, I was facing a new kind of hurt. A deeper cut.

My mom didn't smoke, and she tried to keep up her appearance, but she looked frail. She had that addict's look, powder clinging to her nose hairs, constant sniffing, and that far-off stare that always made me cringe.

I don't know if she was buying from the boys at my school or if they just recognized the signs. Either way, her addiction followed me through those halls like a shadow.

And the kids? Mean as hell.

Somehow, even through the teasing, I was still considered one of the popular girls. Some boys liked me. Some bullied me. Some did both.

That was my life, balance inside chaos.

That's when I got my next nickname.

Rock Baby.

As in crack baby.

As in your mama's a dope fiend.

The worst of them was a boy named Keith. He never used my real name. It was always Rock Baby.

At school, I rolled my eyes and pretended it didn't touch me.

At home, I cried into my pillow some nights and my heart thudded like fists against my ribs.

Some days I hated him.

Most days, I hated her.

I begged my mom to stop showing up high. I told her she could keep using, just don't let them see. I couldn't take the teasing anymore.

Imagine being a child, begging your mother not for sobriety, but for shame.

By then, my fuse was already blown. My pennies had already flown. My rage wasn't new. And I didn't have the tools to fix myself.

Emotional intelligence wasn't just lacking in action. It was lacking in knowledge.

I told my mother the next time I was called "Rock Baby", I was going to explode. I warned her she would have to come up to the school. I was tired of the name-calling. It was embarrassing, humiliating, and it really hurt my feelings to be called that name in front of everyone who laughed and no one who felt sorry for me.

One day, next time came.

We were in science class. There was a green chalkboard, the desks were positioned in rows, the dusty smell of old books and overhead lights buzzing faintly. I could hear the clock ticking, louder than it should've been.

The teacher asked for volunteers to answer questions. I stood up, answered a question correctly. For a second, I felt proud. Like I was more than what they called me.

Then I heard it.

"Good job, Rock Baby."

That was it.

Not today. Not again.

This was the moment I'd warned my mother about. It wasn't rehearsed, but my bomb had already been set. Hearing his words made it explode.

The words pounded in my head.

I slid my chair back, screeching across the floor. I picked up that plastic seat, its cold silver legs trembling in my sweaty grip. I stood over Keith's head, ready.

"I'm sick of your ass. Call me Rock Baby again and I'm going to knock your fucking head off. Say it again. I dare you."

Silence hovered over the entire classroom.

Keith was also silent. He had the same look of fear I'd seen on my mama's face the day I threw those pennies.

Everyone froze.

Because I wasn't bluffing.

I still had the chair raised. The tears burning my eyes. My arms were shaking. My adrenaline was rushing. But the courage to execute my plan showed up confidently. I was ready to risk it all.

Then.

"LaTanya," Ms. Foster said calmly, "go to the counselor's office."

Not the principal's office.

Not detention.

Not suspension.

Even after the cursing, the threat, the chair. She sent me to the counselor, someone who could help.

I was already crying and shaking. Then everything hit me at once.

I lost control of my emotions again, this time I wasn't in the comforts of my home. I was at school!

I cried as I stormed down to her office. I didn't care who saw me.

In that office, I told her I was sick of all the people who called me Rock Baby and all the people who laughed at me.

I also told her about all the boys who sold drugs in my class. I told her how they hid their stash in the bottom parts of their pencil sharpeners in their lockers.

Keith was a young distributor, a drug dealer, and someone who sold drugs to people like my mother.

The fact that he was the ringleader baffled me. He was pushing out the drugs the parents used, and he had the nerve to tease me.

She just listened with understanding and care.

And in that moment, wiping snot on my sleeve, my chest still heaving, I thought maybe I wasn't this crazy kid who had no emotional control. Maybe someone finally saw past the nickname, past my mama's shame, past my own rage.

She knew what I needed wasn't discipline.

She knew I needed to be seen and heard.

After that day, something changed. I was no longer called Rock Baby.

Looking back, it's a shame that I had to go to the extremes of cursing and threatening somebody with a chair just to be left alone.

Do I regret it? Absolutely not.

Would I encourage somebody else to rage out like that? Not really.

But that was my way, and it got me the respect I deserved.

Kids act mean and tough, but even a bully knew when enough was enough.

TRUTH BE TOLD

Truth be told, sometimes it isn't rocket science. It's simple cause and effect.

A parent's addiction can create cracks in a child's world, and bullies are quick to find those cracks and press into them.

The teasing, the whispers, the shame of being labeled because of a parent's choices, it all adds up.

It doesn't take much for a child to snap when they've carried too much for too long.

Recognizing how the weight of bullying and family chaos can collide is the first step in breaking the cycle.

It's not rocket science. It's the truth.

When pain piles up, it demands to be felt; and more importantly, it deserves to be healed.

Even kids deserve to heal and to be seen beyond the hurt they've carried.

LET'S DO THE HEART WORK:
It's Not Rocket Science

Take your time reflecting on these questions in your journal. Allow your heart to speak honestly. Healing is not a race; it is your right.

The Heart Work For
Adult Children Of Addicts

When you think about your childhood, what moments of chaos shaped your view of yourself?

- Write down 2-3 specific memories.
- How did you feel in those moments?
- How do these memories affect your choices today?

What nicknames or labels have you carried that were given to you by others?

- Do they still affect your confidence or self-talk today?
- List the labels or nicknames you remember.
- How do they make you feel now?
- What new truth would you like to replace them with?

What would you tell your younger self who was trying to find stability in chaos?

- Write a short letter to your younger self.
- What would you want them to know about safety and hope?

The Heart Work for Parents in Recovery

Reflect on a time when your actions may have impacted your child's school experience. How do you think your child felt?

- Describe the situation from your child's perspective.
- What do you wish you could have done differently?

How can you support your child's healing, even if you are still on your own healing journey?

- Write down small, consistent actions you can take to show support.
- How can you show your child you see them and are willing to grow?

BREATH BREAK BEFORE YOU CONTINUE

Before moving into your next chapter or reflection, take a **Breath Break** to honor your body and spirit:

- Sit comfortably and place one hand on your heart, one hand on your belly.
- Inhale deeply through your nose for a count of 4, hold for a count of 4, and exhale slowly through your mouth for a count of 6.
- As you breathe, say quietly to yourself: *"I am safe. I am allowed to rest. I am allowed to heal."*
- Repeat this breathing cycle three times, letting your shoulders drop with each exhale.
- Allow yourself to notice any tension you are holding and give yourself permission to release it.

When you are ready, thank yourself for showing up to your heart work, and continue your journey at your own gentle pace.

"Scars are not signs of weakness. They are proof you survived." —
Unknown

CHAPTER SEVEN: A Chain Reaction

The story of how addiction can turn into a chain reaction of unfortunate and memorable events.

It was the summer of 1993. I had just graduated eighth grade. A few weeks before my graduation, I found out my father had gone back to jail. Again.

Of course, that meant he didn't make it to my graduation.

I remember standing there in my cap and gown, looking at all the dads who showed up, wishing mine could see me walk across that stage. Wishing he would have told me he was proud of me, the way he always did.

My mom, John, and I were still living in our ugly little basement apartment. The one that smelled like Raid, incense, and that cheap Walgreens spray, Primo.

Just to the right of the living room was my mother's bedroom. To the left, a dark laundry room with no working light. The bathroom was next, dingy, windowless, with cracked tile and yellowish plastic around the tub. And beyond that, at the very back, was the bedroom I shared with John. The same room my Uncle Bobby had stayed in with us before he took his life.

The walls were wrapped in brown paneling, and wedged between our room and the bathroom sat a greenish-yellow vinyl chair, cracked wide open at the seat, exposing the white cushion underneath. I never understood why we kept that chair. But it had claimed its corner, so there it stayed.

One afternoon, I came in from outside to take a break from the summer heat. I had on my blue Karl Kani shirt with the matching baggy Karl Kani shorts, my favorite outfit at the time. In the '90s, it didn't matter if the outfit came from 63rd and Halsted or Evergreen Plaza, a Karl Kani outfit made a statement.

Before this, I wore my herringbone chain to The Rink on Saturday nights, from seven to eleven. The music loud, the lights swirling, my chain catching the glow as I danced... feeling important. Feeling like something in a world that often made me feel less than.

My mom was home, and I could tell something was off the second I walked in. The air felt heavier, like it was holding its breath.

She didn't just look high. She looked sick. Sweating, pacing, scratching at her arms. Anxious while still trying to look calm, in a way that felt more physical than emotional. By this time, I knew what it meant to be dope sick. And that was the vibe she was giving.

She motioned for me to sit down.

I sat in that cracked vinyl chair, not thinking about how the cushion would dig into my legs until I felt the sharp tears in the plastic scratch against my skin. The chair creaked beneath me, the sound echoing louder than it should've in that small hallway.

She stood in front of me, shifting from foot to foot, then sat on the stairs that led to the house upstairs, her eyes darting around the room like she was trying to figure out how to say what she needed to say.

She cleared her throat and started explaining how pawning worked. How you could take something in, get cash for it, and if you paid it back within a week, they'd give it back to you.

Then she paused, and her eyes finally met mine.

"Tanya, I just need it for a little while, okay? Just until Friday. I promise I'll get it right back."

And then it hit me. What she was asking.

She wanted to pawn my herringbone chain. The one I'd gotten for my fourteenth birthday. A gift to celebrate graduating eighth grade. A big-deal chain. A real one. Thick enough to show. Heavy enough to hold pride.

I sat there, silent.

My hands clenched in my lap, fingernails pressing half-moons into my palms. I rested my head against the paneling as I looked up at the uncovered and unpainted beams in the ceiling.

This wasn't the first time she'd taken something from someone. She'd pawned her own things before. Stolen from my grandparents, even. I knew this wasn't just a favor. It was a cycle. But at least this time she asked.

"I don't want to give it up," I whispered, my voice cracking as tears welled up, my head still toward the ceiling to keep them from falling.

It was Friday, and I wanted to wear my chain to The Rink. I wanted to feel good. I wanted to feel seen. The chain made me feel like something. And here she was, asking me to give that something up for a hit.

But I also understood.

I understood what withdrawal did to her body. I understood what it looked like when she was desperate, pacing and living in a hell she couldn't escape from. I was outspoken by then. I had thrown pennies, snapped at boy at school, let my emotions take the wheel more than once. But even with all that fire in me, I couldn't tell her no.

Because in all her madness, she still took care of me. Plus, she often gave me tips on my appearance, my hair, and my hygiene.

Because underneath the pain, I loved my mother.

Because deep down, I didn't want her to suffer.

Because I just didn't have the courage. Not yet.

I reached behind my neck, feeling the cool metal of the clasp beneath my trembling fingers. For a moment, I hesitated. The metal was cold and familiar. My breath caught as I looked at her and saw the need in her eyes swallowing everything else.

Then I unclasped the chain.

And handed it to her.

She took it quickly, clutching it like it was her last lifeline, her hands shaking as she tucked it into her pocket.

She didn't say thank you. She promised she'd get it back. She didn't have to, though.

She turned and walked out the door, her shoulders hunched, her thin arms swinging stiffly, her hair not curled, just slicked back with gel and mousse as she hurried up those five stairs and out that ugly green cracked door.

I listened to the soft slap of her flip-flops against the concrete, the screen door creaked, then slammed, leaving behind a sharp, empty silence. I went to my room, buried my face in the pillow, and cried myself to sleep, waking up the next morning chainless.

A week later, she gave it back to me. Holding it out with a bright, shaky smile like she was giving it to me for the first time.

Maybe she was just proud she kept her word. The chain was still intact. But something important about it had changed. Not the shape. But everything it meant to me.

I wore it, but not with pride anymore. The shine was still there, but the joy wasn't.

It had become a symbol of sacrifice. Of how love and survival had started to look like the same thing.

When herringbone chains fell out of style, I stopped wearing it.

But the weight of it never really left me.

That chain still hangs around my story. Not around my neck, but in the place where I first learned what it costs to say yes when you want to scream no.

TRUTH BE TOLD

Truth be told, I've learned that addiction doesn't end its impact just because a parent gets clean. The past doesn't disappear. It lives inside the child who had to carry the weight of their parent's choices.

It creates a chain reaction. One moment of watching a parent's sickness. One day of having to give something up. One time of saying yes when we wanted to scream no. Each moment links to the next, shaping how we learn to trust, how we learn to protect ourselves, and how we learn to love.

Even after recovery comes, the memories don't vanish. They stay with us, woven into our stories.

But seeing this chain reaction for what it is gives us a chance to understand ourselves and where some of our pain started. It gives us the power to break that chain, piece by piece, so we can stop carrying what was never ours to hold.

LET'S DO THE HEART WORK:
A Chain Reaction

These questions are here to help you understand your story with compassion, to honor your experiences, and to take small steps toward freedom and deeper connection. Be gentle with yourself as you write.

The Heart Work For
Adult Children Of Addicts

What is a time you had to give up or lost something important to you because of your parent's addiction?

- Write about the item and why it was important to you.
- Describe how it felt when it was taken.
- Reflect on what you wish could have happened instead and what you need now to heal.

When did you feel you had to say "yes" when you really wanted to say "no"?

- Describe the situation and what you were afraid would happen if you said "no".
- Share how it felt in your body to say "yes" when you wanted to say "no".
- Reflect on what you wish you could have said or done differently.

What did you lose or give up to keep peace or help your parent?

- Write about what you gave up and how it affected you.
- Describe what you wanted to say but couldn't at that time.
- Reflect on how you can reclaim what was lost now.

The Heart Work for Parents in Recovery

Was there ever a time you asked your child to give up something or you took something important so you could meet a need in your addiction?

- Describe what you asked for and why.
- Reflect on what you believe your child felt in that moment.
- Write what you would say to your child about that moment.

How did your addiction affect your ability to be present for your child's sense of pride and belonging?

- Share a time when your child was excited about something important to them.
- Reflect on how your addiction impacted your response or presence.
- Write about how you would like to support your child's sense of pride now.

What can you do now to acknowledge the moments your child sacrificed to help you when you were struggling?

- List one or two ways you can express gratitude to your child.
- Reflect on how you can show your child you see their sacrifices.
- Write about what accountability and healing look like for you today.

BREATH BREAK BEFORE YOU CONTINUE

Before moving into your next chapter or reflection, take a **Breath Break** to honor your body and spirit:

- Sit comfortably and place one hand on your heart, one hand on your belly.
- Inhale deeply through your nose for a count of 4, hold for a count of 4, and exhale slowly through your mouth for a count of 6.
- As you breathe, say quietly to yourself: *"I am safe. I am allowed to rest. I am allowed to heal."*
- Repeat this breathing cycle three times, letting your shoulders drop with each exhale.
- Allow yourself to notice any tension you are holding and give yourself permission to release it.

When you are ready, thank yourself for showing up to your heart work, and continue your journey at your own gentle pace.

Every step you take toward healing, no matter how small, is a revolution."
— Unknown

CHAPTER EIGHT: Such A Dope Idea

The story of how addiction shapes bad decisions, even in your home.

It was 1994 when we moved out of the basement apartment. If I remember right, we were asked to leave and given a deadline to be out. My mom found us a new place, and that's when things started to go from bad to worse.

The house was small but cute, a little beige and brown box tucked back on seventy-eighth and St. Lawrence. It looked like a coach house, except there wasn't a main house in front. Just a single, lonely unit set far back from the street, hidden behind a few bushes. Easier to reach from the alley than the sidewalk.

The front steps creaked when you walked up them. In summer, the yard smelled like hot grass, dust, and oil from the neighbor's driveway that lined up with our walkway.

What I loved most about that house was having the basement to myself. It felt like my own tiny apartment. My space smelled faintly damp, like old concrete and laundry soap. I didn't have to be upstairs, face-to-face with my mom, her boyfriend at the time, or the steady stream of visitors drifting in and out of her bedroom. It gave me peace, privacy, and a sliver of normal life I could hide inside.

The house only had one bathroom, squeezed beside her room, so that was really the only time I had to interact with the adults.

The layout was weird but familiar. Step through the front door, and John's room was on the left. To the right, a living room just big enough for a loveseat. Past that was a narrow doorway with the bathroom and a small sitting area where we squeezed in the rest of our furniture and a dusty TV on a wobbly stand.

The kitchen was small, with the stove, fridge, and sink lined up on the left, and old wooden cabinets on the right that we painted brown. They smelled like a mix of spices and mildew. The basement stairs were tucked beside those cabinets and creaked every time I tiptoed down to my hideaway.

Granny's house wasn't close enough to just pop over, but I could walk there if I had to. I didn't love that. But my best friend lived right around the corner. We even shared alleys, so that helped. It was the kind of setup where things could've been better, but they also could've been worse.

At our new place, my mother let me come and go as I pleased. I didn't have to look after John as much. I didn't ask to go anywhere, I just told her. She allowed me to have boys in my room and even let my boyfriend live there for a bit during my senior year.

The thought of it now makes my stomach twist. How does a parent do that? How does a mother make space for her child's boyfriend but not her child? She handed over any shred of responsibility just to keep me out of her way. Looking back, I see it for what it was. Neglect, disguised as freedom. A girl left to figure out boundaries on her own, in a house where there weren't any.

Even though she didn't set rules, I still stayed respectful in my own ways. I always came home at a decent hour. I never stayed out without telling her where I'd be. And I carried myself in a way that demanded respect because I understood early on that if I didn't, no one else would.

I had plenty of friends. My mother had plenty so called friends of her own. Faces drifted in and out, and many of the names I never bothered to learn. But one stuck: Katrice.

Katrice was younger than my mom by about ten years and older than me by the same. She dealt drugs, probably connected through the dealer we all knew from the neighborhood. Katrice had the supply. My mom had the hunger.

They started hanging out more. Katrice liked me though and I thought she was cool, in her own way. She'd always make sure my mom looked out for me, she even did my nails for prom. I remember them turning out lumpy, crooked, and overall hideous.

But even small kindnesses don't change the truth. The people my mother let into our world weren't harmless. They all served a purpose. Supply or getting high. None of them were people I'd have around my family.

My mother spent a lot of time at Katrice's place. One day, something went down over there. I overheard my mom on the phone, her voice low and sharp, talking about drugs all over Katrice's living room and some big mistake with the supplier. He wasn't happy and decided to shut down her operation.

When Katrice's operation got cancelled, I guess something clicked for my mom. I don't know what deal she made, but somehow our house became the new spot.

Thanks to her habit, there were never any big stashes kept there. Just a system that worked for them.

That summer in 1997, right after I graduated high school, things shifted in our house.

I remember being so excited because I'd just gotten my own phone line installed in the basement. I thought it was a gift. Something my mom did just for me so I could gossip with my friends for hours without her yelling at me to get off the line.

It wasn't.

Two nights after I gave my number to every friend I had, the phone rang at 2 a.m. My eyes were half-shut with sleep as I groped for the receiver, the cold cord brushing my bare shoulder.

"Hello?"

"Hey, is this Camelot?"

"Uh… no, you got the wrong number."

"This is Camelot. Ain't this Camelot? I'm tryna get some dope. This the number they gave me."

I was pissed.

And just like that, it wasn't mine anymore. Not the number. Not the phone. Not the one thing I thought was given to me as a gift.

I slammed the receiver down so hard it bounced. I stormed up the basement stairs, I skipped two at a time, my feet pounded so loud I felt them in my teeth. I banged on her door until my knuckles stung. She opened it with heavy eyelids and a lazy apology; she said she was sorry, that it wouldn't happen again.

She was right. It didn't. Because the line had done its job.

That phone line wasn't mine. It never was. It had never been a gift. It was just another tool, another corner cut to keep her addiction running smoothly. That call wasn't a mistake. It was a sign. I wasn't living in my own space anymore. I was living in a house where my privacy, my safety, didn't matter. Not to her.

A few days later, I dragged myself upstairs one morning to use the bathroom. The air was warm and smelled of an unfamiliar cologne that didn't belong to anyone in our house. To my surprise, one of the dope boys, someone I'd seen around before but never really noticed, was slouched on our couch like he had been living there for weeks. The TV flickered across his face as he flipped through channels with one hand and crushed a half-empty bag of chips against his knee with the other.

I froze halfway into the living room, eyes squinted, toes curling into the plush brown carpet.

"What are you doing here?" I asked, trying to make my voice louder than the alarm ringing in my chest.

He glanced at me, then back at the TV like I was the guest.

"They didn't tell you?" He shrugged, smirking around a mouthful of chips. "I'm just here taking care of some business."

Before I could answer, there was a knock at the back door. Two taps, a pause, three more.

I turned to open it, but he held up a finger while he finished chewing.

"Nah," he said, pushing himself up with a grunt. "Don't get the door. That's what I'm here for."

He opened the back door like he'd done it a hundred times. I heard low voices, the rustle of cash, the quiet clink of something metal. A moment later, the door closed, and he dropped back on the couch, wiping his fingers on his jeans.

Then he looked at me with concern as if he was more confused than I was.

"Are you okay?" he asked, his voice gentle.

"I guess," I said, because what else could I say.

He studied me for a moment, eyes steady. Not like a dope boy handling business. More like a big brother I didn't ask for.

"You cool, for real," he said. "You live here? Is your mom Rita? I didn't know you were living like this."

He didn't mean the house. He meant the life.

And he wasn't wrong.

I stood there a minute, arms crossed over my robe, holding it closed, wondering how a stranger could try to respect me when my mother didn't.

That's what stuck with me. Not the phone line. Not the strangers at our door. Not even the deals being made in whispers behind my back. It was the way my mother handed me over to this world without saying a word. Like my safety wasn't worth mentioning. Like my peace wasn't worth keeping.

And still, the operation didn't stop. It became normal. Part of my routine.

Some days, I sat up with the guys who came to serve. We'd talk about music, basketball, or people in the neighborhood. Just regular people killing time. They never made me feel unsafe. Never hit on me.

One of the guys, medium build, low haircut, always in a button-up, was cool. He gave me advice about boys and told stories about the women he dated. When I saw him outside, we'd nod at each other like we shared a secret nobody else would understand. My friends never asked how I knew him, and I never told.

Those small talks, while the house buzzed with something darker, were a strange comfort in my chaotic world. It was one of the cracks where God slipped in to cover me, even when it didn't make sense for me to be safe.

Different guys came like clockwork, eight in the morning to six in the evening, like they were punching in for a nine-to-five. Always polite. Always business. Somehow, that made it worse. It turned my living room into a quiet waiting room for a life I didn't choose.

Downstairs, I pretended to be a regular teenager. I blasted my music to drown out the footsteps upstairs. I danced around my small room, twirling the cord of the phone that wasn't really mine anymore, scribbling secrets in my diary while dope changed hands upstairs.

When I walked through the hallway or passed the back door, I kept my eyes forward, like I was moving through smoke I had learned not to see. Outside, I laughed and hung out with my friends like nothing was different.

Nobody knew that inside, I was living between reality and a trap house.

Because what was I supposed to say? That while people clocked in for work, my house was clocking in junkies. That while kids rode bikes down the street, grown men knocked at my back door for a fix. That I learned to act normal in a house that could've been raided at any moment.

Eventually, that operation ended. By then, it had become so normal I barely noticed. I had learned to tune it out. That was survival. Not choice.

My mom and I never had a real conversation about why she felt it was a good idea to run the operation out of our house. I'm just grateful nothing worse happened.

That house, and the things I lived with there, taught me something I didn't expect.

You can find peace in the middle of a storm.
You can be protected even when it doesn't make sense.
You can stand in chaos and still come out whole.

Truth Be Told

Truth be told, that part of my life wasn't really about survival. Not for me, anyway. It was about my mother's survival. Her way of making fast money. Her way of keeping her habit close and her responsibilities far away.

She thought turning our house into a dope spot was a good idea. I see now how broken you have to be to think something like that makes sense.

But in the middle of her "dope idea," I had to come up with my own. My idea was survival. My idea was learning how to hold on to myself in a house that felt like it was slipping away.

The truth is, I did survive. Not because of her, but in spite of her. And it was Such a Dope Idea for me to do the normal things I did. That house was a reminder that even when you're handed someone else's chaos, you still get to decide how the story ends.

LET'S DO THE HEART WORK:
Such A Dope Idea

These questions are here to help you understand your story with compassion, to honor your experiences, and to take small steps toward freedom and deeper connection. Be gentle with yourself as you write.

The Heart Work For
Adult Children of Addicts

What did it feel like to live in a house where you had to pretend everything was normal?

- What were moments when you felt safest or found small comforts in chaos?
- How did pretending impact your ability to trust your feelings?
- What does "normal" mean to you now?

What helped you survive in a situation you didn't choose?

- Was it faith, music, friends, writing, or something else?
- Do you still use those survival tools now?
- How did those tools shape your resilience?

The Heart Work for Parents in Recovery

What "dope ideas" did you think were helping you survive but hurt your children?

- Are there choices you made that you now see differently in recovery?
- How did those choices affect your relationship with your children?
- How can you acknowledge those choices while also forgiving yourself?

How do you define "home" now in your recovery journey?

- What does safety look like for you and your family today?
- What would you like your children to feel when they think about home now?
- What steps can you take to repair or redefine home for yourself and your children?

How can you help your children process the chaos they experienced?

- Are there conversations you need to have with them to acknowledge the past?
- How can you create space for your children to share their truth safely?
- What can you do to show your children you are present and committed to change?

BREATH BREAK BEFORE YOU CONTINUE

Before moving into your next chapter or reflection, take a **Breath Break** to honor your body and spirit:

- Sit comfortably and place one hand on your heart, one hand on your belly.
- Inhale deeply through your nose for a count of 4, hold for a count of 4, and exhale slowly through your mouth for a count of 6.
- As you breathe, say quietly to yourself: *"I am safe. I am allowed to rest. I am allowed to heal."*
- Repeat this breathing cycle three times, letting your shoulders drop with each exhale.
- Allow yourself to notice any tension you are holding and give yourself permission to release it.

When you are ready, thank yourself for showing up to your heart work, and continue your journey at your own gentle pace.

"Scars are not signs of weakness.
They are proof you survived."
— Unknown

CHAPTER NINE: Angel In Disguise

The story of how my mother's life changed for good in the most unexpected way, by two people who had her fate in their hands.

As you may remember, my mom's addiction to heroin started when she was just fifteen years old. For me, that meant every part of my childhood, and nearly all of my teenage years, was shaped by her drug use. I didn't grow up learning about addiction from the outside. I saw it up close and personal.

Before my little brother John was born, I already had clear memories of going with my mom to methadone clinics. I was still young, too young to understand anything, but old enough to start remembering everything.

One clinic stands out in my memory. It was a small building tucked inside Bronzeville in Chicago. Back then, living in Bronzeville didn't carry the meaning or the home prices it carries today.

Inside, the clinic had a dull glow, like the windows hadn't seen sunlight in years. The pinkish-red carpet in the waiting area was worn down to black in high-traffic spots. Vinyl chairs lined the walls, some back-to-back, some facing each other. Most were beige and red with cracked seats that pinched your legs if you shifted.

My mom would sign in, and we'd sit and wait. When they called her name, I could go with her. The staff was always kind. Maybe because I was the only kid in there.

Everyone waited for what I thought was orange juice in a small plastic cup with a white lid. I even asked once if I could have some.

A woman smiled sadly and said, "Oh no, sweetie. You definitely don't want this. This isn't for kids."

Some time later, I learned more about methadone, a legal opioid meant to help people wean off heroin. The same drug I had to withdraw from when I was born.

Looking back, I never fully understood why my mom took methadone and still used heroin. I'll just add that to the list of things I don't need to know.

For the first nineteen years of my life, there were several times she tried to kick her habit.

Whenever my mom wanted to get sober, she would check herself into 30-day rehab programs. I remember at least three different times when she did that. During those stints, Granny would keep John and me. Before she went in, my mom would warn me that we couldn't talk for at least a week. Later, I found out it was because detox was too rough.

Through my own research and by listening to adult conversations, I learned that heroin withdrawal isn't just painful. It's brutal. It's like watching someone's body turn against them. One minute they're freezing, the next they're sweating buckets, legs shaking, stomach in knots, throwing up, unable to keep anything down, unable to sleep, unable to get comfortable no matter what. Every bone in their body hurts.

There were also mood swings. Snapping, begging, crying, desperate for the same dope they were trying to escape. There's an emptiness in their eyes and barely any life in their bodies when the high is gone. The days feel long, and the nights even longer. Once they get past withdrawal, they're usually better... until the craving becomes stronger than the desire to want better for themselves.

And the cycle starts over again.

I used to think that going through withdrawal once would be enough pain to keep someone clean. But now I understand, withdrawal is only the beginning. A person has to do a lot more if they want to stay free.

Out of all the rehab facilities my mom visited, there was one place I'll never forget. It was a rehab center called Interventions on the West Side of Chicago, near Lake Street. A brick building with lots of windows. From the outside, it looked dingy, but inside, it was surprisingly clean. The floors were hard and cold. The white walls made it feel like a hospital with no nurses.

My mom shared a small room with another woman. There were two twin beds with wooden headboards and footboards, pushed up against opposite walls near a window. Her side of the room was neat, with just a few books and a Bible on the nightstand.

Outside that window was a small grassy area where people would walk their dogs or sit reading under trees. It felt calm and safe.

After the room tour, my mom, Granny, and I sat in a little family lounge and talked. I don't remember what we said, but I remember how she made promises. How things would change. How it would be different when she came home.

And every single time, I believed her. Because no matter how many times I told her I hated her, I really loved her. And I also had hope.

When her thirty days were up, my mom would come home and appear sober. For a while. A few weeks, maybe. Then the pattern would start again. She'd start messing with her nose, rubbing it, sniffing. A small shift, but to me, it was big.

A few days later, that telltale powder would reappear, clinging to the tiny hairs in her nose like a quiet confession she would never say out loud.

She had relapsed. Again.

I felt hopeless when she relapsed. She was always a better person when she was clean. Granny respected her more. So did I.

But when she was using, my mom would steal from my grandparents. She'd miss family gatherings. She'd become the person my cousins laughed at. And I always carried the shame.

Living life as an addict and doing whatever it takes to support a habit comes with consequences. Distrust from family members. Being accused of stealing whatever went missing. And for some, it means getting caught.

It means jail.

There were several short stints where my mom's theft landed her in Cook County Jail. I remember those trips with my grandmother. My mother was in Division 3. There was no parking lot. Just cracked streets and parallel parking if you were lucky. So we'd walk the rest of the way, past the barbed wire curling like thorns above us.

Inside, it wasn't just metal detectors. There were guards barking at us like we were criminals too.

"No belts. No metal. Take the change out of your pocket."

They were loud for no reason. Mean just because they could be.

We sat in a waiting area painted in some kind of dirty yellow, like the walls themselves had absorbed every sad story that passed through them. Orange plastic chairs bolted to the floor. Nothing soft. Nothing kind.

When they called "Beasley," we stood up and were guided to the visiting room by a guard. Inside were about six stools lined up like punishments. There was thick glass between us and the people we loved. We communicated on dirty phones with cracked cords, the kind of cracks you imagine a thousand desperate fingers had tried to pull free.

I couldn't touch her. Couldn't hold her hand. Couldn't cry in front of her.

So, I waited.

I didn't wait until we got to the car either. I held those tears like a secret all the way home.

That feeling, of a young girl seeing her mother in jail, was tormenting.

I remember that same feeling a few years earlier. Back in the 80s, my paternal grandparents took me to see my father in the same jail. Different building, same entrance. Same cold feeling in my stomach when we left.

Back then, I would cry all the way home.

When parents go to jail, I understand how important it is for them to see their kids while they're locked up. But I don't think they consider the emotional strain, the nightmares, and the emptiness a child feels during those visits.

A child leaves not knowing if they'll ever hug or talk to their parent face to face again.

Even with those feelings, I remember going back to see my mother again. Same routine. Same sad feeling. Same emptiness when I left. But I toughed it out.

Looking back, my mother went to jail for theft and forgery... each time was one time too many.

Every time she came home, from jail or rehab, I had hope. Hope that maybe she'd been clean during those times away. Hope that maybe she wouldn't go back. But the cycle always came around again. She would start rubbing her nose. Then the residue would reappear. Like a clock striking relapse.

I didn't understand addiction fully back then. To me, it looked like a choice. I thought going to jail would be enough to scare someone straight. Now I know addiction is a disease. And if the wound isn't fully treated, the relapse isn't far behind.

There had been a stretch where my mom stayed out of legal trouble. Until she didn't.

When we were living on seventy-eighth and St. Lawrence, she got mixed up with new people. They didn't help her get clean. They helped her get more dope. And more trouble.

After everything I had seen, I was tired. Numb. I had lost respect for her.

I coined a phrase I used to tell her all the time:
"Respect is like a boomerang. If you don't throw it out, you don't get it back."

I meant that then. I still do now.

Between the dope house, the people she brought around, that bedroom door always being closed, and stepping on those curling irons she never turned off, I was just tired of her mess.

I would go into rages, tear up the house, throw things. I would also write notes at night and leave them on the old dusty TV for her to find in the morning.

One day during my senior year of high school, right before I left for school, I remember writing a note about how bad she looked. By that time, she was extremely thin. Her skin had darkened, and no matter how much she tried to keep herself together, she looked like a dope fiend. I was embarrassed by her. I told her I didn't want her at my senior graduation. I wanted what was known at Ruggles to stay a secret at CVS.

In that note, I wrote:
"You look like a stick that fell off a tree, gained life, and started walking around."

Today I can laugh. But back then, it wasn't funny. It was mean. And it was also sad. But I didn't care.

She looked so bad to me that I was embarrassed to even see her in the house. I was also sick of her messing up the public aid check as soon as she got it. I needed money. And I needed to not depend on her anymore.

At seventeen, right before my senior year, I got my first job at Jewel Food Store on 75th and Stony Island. Eighty dollars a week after union dues and health insurance. That check felt like freedom. No more waiting on a once-a-month public aid check.

No more urine-smelling waiting rooms at the public aid doctor's office.

I had somewhere to go.

The first day I started my job, I remember coming home from school to rest before orientation. I laid across the couch and tried to relax. After a short while, I felt something unusual on my leg. Then it started to sting.

I jumped up fast and realized what had happened.

Those curling irons. Still on. Still hot. Just sitting on a towel like that made it safe.

Without thinking, I had rested my leg on them. The burn was instant. It left a long, deep blister that throbbed all day. Still, I went to work and did what I had to do. I treated it the best I could.

That scar never left. It became a kind of war wound, a reminder of where I came from and why I had to leave.

Outside of that, the job at Jewel saved me. It gave me a break from the house, from the mess, from the anger I couldn't always control. It gave me a reason to leave, and a reason to stay gone.

One day, my mom showed up at my job. Her hair wasn't combed. Her clothes didn't match. She looked sick and out of place. I could see she needed money, and I could tell she didn't care who saw her asking for it.

I was ringing up customers, doing my best to look like I belonged there. I looked up, and there she was. Walking toward me like this was something normal. Like she wasn't about to embarrass me.

My heart dropped. My face got hot. I was humiliated.

I gave her the money just to get her to go away. Then I told her not to ever come to my job again.

At our house, things kept spiraling. A few months after the Camelot operation stopped, the house got cold. Literally cold.

We called a maintenance guy to come light the pilot. When he got there, we found out the truth.

The gas had been shut off.

No gas meant no heat. No hot water. No cooking.

My mom wasn't home that day. She came in briefly and said she would be back later.

Later never came.

She had done something. It landed her in jail again. This time it was forgery. Her bond was too high for anyone to pay. She wasn't going anywhere.

And neither were we.

The phone got disconnected next. I started walking to 79th near Pride Cleaners just to use a payphone. I showered at Granny's or at a friend's house. But I still slept in that cold house until the eviction notice showed up.

With my mom still in jail, John and I packed up and moved back in with Granny.

About a month later, my mother had a court date. I didn't go. I had stopped visiting her on visiting days too. I was angry. I was embarrassed. I was tired of seeing her behind glass.

She had been assigned a public defender. And somehow, that woman ended up being an angel in disguise.

I was told that the public defender looked over my mother's history. Maybe she saw the pattern. Maybe she saw something the rest of the world overlooked. She didn't argue that my mother was innocent. She told the truth.

"This woman doesn't need to be institutionalized," she said. "She's an addict. She needs help."

And for once, the judge agreed.

That was something the rest of us had always known but had no power to enforce. Instead of jail, my mom was sent to a recovery program. She was eventually released on house arrest and required to drop regularly to prove she was staying clean.

For a while, she was. Then the pattern began to shift again. She started hanging out with the same people. Skipped meetings. Rubbing her nose again. And I knew.

I always knew.

On July 16, 1998, she had another court date. That morning, she woke me up and asked if I would come with her and Granny.

I told her no.

It was the same no I should have given her the day she asked for my chain.

That no was my way of protecting myself. I knew she had relapsed. I knew she wasn't coming home. I couldn't watch her go back to jail again.

In my heart, I hoped I was wrong. But I wasn't.

Later that day, Granny came home alone. My mom wasn't with her. My stomach was in knots. I already knew what had happened.

Granny sat down on the wicker sofa in the den and called my name.

"LaTanya."

I sat on the floor in front of her, my hands moving slowly through the plush pink carpet.

She started crying.

"They kept Renee," she said through tears. "Oh Lord... they kept Renee."

I knew it. I had been right to protect myself. But hearing it still broke something in me.

I hugged Granny. She told me not to worry, that John and I would be okay.

I didn't cry right then. I hugged her again and left for work.

At the store, I was a cashier, doing my best to keep it together while ringing up customers. But the tears I had tucked away started to surface. I closed my lane, rushed to the employee bathroom, and let them out.

I cried hard.

The kind of cry that empties you.

Eventually, I pulled myself together and told my boss I needed to leave.

When she asked why, I held back the tears and said, "My mom had court today. The judge kept her. I don't know when she's coming back."

Her face softened. The irritation disappeared. It was replaced with a kind of concern I wasn't used to getting from adults.

"Oh LaTanya," she said. "That is horrible."

She hugged me and let me clock out.

I went home. I laid down. And I cried myself to sleep.

Just like I did the night I gave her my chain.

Just like I did when we left the jail.

Except this time, I wasn't crying because of her.

I was crying for her.

Because July 16, 1998, was the last day my mother ever used drugs.

She was sent to Haymarket House near Harpo Studios for treatment. When I visited her, she looked younger, happier, and cleaner than I'd ever seen her.

This time, she didn't make promises.

She just talked about the future.

She completed the program. When she came home, she started going to meetings. She changed her habits. She distanced herself from the people who used to keep her stuck.

She finally replaced the three things every recovering addict has to change.

People. Places. And things.

Where she is now

My mother didn't just stay clean. She rebuilt her life in ways that still inspire me.

A few years into her sobriety, I was still working at Jewel. I remember her coming up to my job, and this time, I proudly introduced her to all of my co-workers. One of my proudest moments that day was introducing her to my boss; the same woman who embraced me and let me go home early the day I broke down after my mom went to jail.

My mother kept going to her meetings. She got her first job at an agency in the social service field and found a passion for helping others. Maybe because for so many years, she had been a burden to people. Now she wanted to give something back.

While working at the agency, she started thinking about advancing in the company. Eventually, she brought up the idea of going back to school. I remember her mentioning college like it was a dream that lived far away.

I told her, "Ma, you've been sober for a while now. You can do anything you put your mind to."

She took those words to heart.

In 2005, she enrolled at Kennedy-King College and earned her Associate of Arts degree in 2007. From there, she kept going. She earned her Bachelor's in Community Health from Chicago State University, then went on to receive her Master's of Science in Nonprofit Management from Spertus College in 2012.

That same year, she walked across the graduation stage with one of her nephews, my cousin. A full circle moment. I watched someone who once mocked my mother's addiction, who had disrespected her, walk side by side with her as they both received their Master's degrees.

My Granny passed away in 2003, but before she left this earth, she got to see my mother clean. I like to believe that when my mother crossed that graduation stage, Granny was smiling down on another proud "Beasley" moment.

Today, my mom is an amazing grandma to John's kids, and to my children, Trinity and Peyton. I'm grateful they only know the version of her she's been for the last twenty-seven years, not the one I had to survive.

I am happy that our children will know that obtaining a degree is possible and it started with, Grandma Rita. My mom's education and accomplishments were never just for herself. They became part of her greater purpose.

My mother has had many full circle inspirational moments. She has shared her story with incarcerated women at Cook County Jail, this time not as an inmate, but as a living testimony of hope. She has spoken to women at Dwight Correctional Center and to audiences as far as Hawaii and Nigeria.

In every room she walks into, she reminds people that healing is possible, recovery is real, and shame doesn't have the final say.

She's still active in the AA community across Chicagoland, continuing to pour into others the way someone once poured into her.

In 2021, my mother and I co-hosted *RecovHERed*, an event we created to bring together mothers and daughters whose relationships had been strained, broken, or reshaped by addiction. It was a beautiful day of healing. Many mothers and daughters experienced vulnerability, understanding, and connection together for the first time.

That day reminded me of what's possible.

Our goal now is to continue doing this work: sharing our story, building our relationship, and reaching others. We want people to know that healing, reconciliation, and restoration are still possible; if you're willing to pray, forgive, and stay open to what's waiting on the other side of pain.

For me, I can't tell my story without naming the truth: drug abuse shaped my childhood. It shaped my anger, my shame, and my heartache.

But I also know this: I wouldn't change a thing.

Everything I went through gave me a testimony I'm proud to tell. It taught me that nobody's story is written in stone based on their worst days. It showed me what forgiveness really looks like. And it gave me something rare, the chance to look at my mother today and see a woman who didn't just get clean, but completely overcame the past.

When you grow up inside addiction, you learn how to lower your expectations. You learn how to survive disappointment. You learn how to read silence. You learn how to smile through pain and plan your escape quietly.

For a long time, I thought that would be our ending: her addiction, my survival, and a silent gap in between.

But God had other plans.

Truth Be Told

Truth be told, recovery didn't just save my mother's life, it gave me a relationship I thought was beyond repair. It gave her to me in a way I never expected. It's not a perfect relationship, not without work, but it's present, whole, and still healing. Every day, she proves that change is possible. Every day, she reminds me that love can survive even the darkest storms.

Looking back, I see how God placed angels in disguise along her path; the public defender, the judge, and all the people who believed in her when she couldn't believe in herself. I believe I was one of them too, without even knowing it, planting seeds of hope even when I was tired, even when I was angry.

Today, when I look at my mother, I don't see addiction. I see strength. I see joy. I see life. I see a woman who was worth saving; a woman who now reaches back to help save others. I see the beauty of what happens when we stop giving up on the people we love, and when we stop giving up on ourselves.

My story isn't just about addiction. It's about hope and faith. And it's about the quiet, everyday miracles that happen when someone shows up at just the right time... as an angel in disguise.

LET'S DO THE HEART WORK:
Angel In Disguise

These questions are here to help you honor where you've been, recognize how far you've come, and take small, meaningful steps toward freedom, healing, and deeper connection. Go gently with yourself as you write. Your story deserves your kindness.

The Heart Work For
Adult Children Of Addicts

What did I lose, and what did I learn?

- List three things you feel you lost growing up around addiction (childhood moments, stability, safety).
- Write down what you learned about yourself because of these losses.
- Consider whether these lessons shaped you in ways you are proud of today.

A moment when I couldn't reach them

- Think of a time when you felt disconnected from your parent because of their addiction. Where were you? What was happening?
- How did it make you feel?
- How has that experience shaped how you trust or connect with people today?

Forgiveness vs. Boundaries

- What does forgiveness mean to you, and how is it different from forgetting?
- Are there boundaries you need to maintain even if you forgive your parent?
- How can you honor your story while also giving yourself permission to live freely?

The Heart Work for Parents in Recovery

The day I realized I needed help

- Describe the moment or day you knew you needed help to get sober.
- What were you most afraid of losing at that moment?
- What did you hope would change if you chose recovery?

My child's perspective

- Imagine how your child may have seen you during your addiction. Write honestly without self-shame.
- What moments do you wish you could explain now?
- How can you show your child through actions that you are different today?

Angels in disguise

- Who were the "angels in disguise" in your recovery journey (a judge, public defender, sponsor, family member)?
- How did their actions impact your path to recovery?
- How can you be an "angel in disguise" to someone else in your recovery community now?

Breath Break Before You Continue

Before moving into your next chapter or reflection, take a **Breath Break** to honor your body and spirit:

- Sit comfortably and place one hand on your heart, one hand on your belly.
- Inhale deeply through your nose for a count of 4, hold for a count of 4, and exhale slowly through your mouth for a count of 6.
- As you breathe, say quietly to yourself: *"I am safe. I am allowed to rest. I am allowed to heal."*
- Repeat this breathing cycle three times, letting your shoulders drop with each exhale.
- Allow yourself to notice any tension you are holding and give yourself permission to release it.

When you are ready, thank yourself for showing up to your heart work, and continue your journey at your own gentle pace.

CHAPTER TEN: My Life

The poem that exposed my pain and everything that happened in between.

<u>My Life</u>

Sometimes I sit and think that my life has no meaning.
Other times, I'd think I was dead, but unfortunately, I was only dreaming.

I'd sit and think why is Uncle Bobby, My Grandma, or other family members are dead.
Why couldn't it be me instead.

Sometimes I wish I had wings so I can fly away from all this heartless pain, and depression.
So now I think it's time to make a confession...

I wish I can get away from all this pain, misery, and doubt,
B-cuz no one sees through these eyes that I see out.

I'm tired of being depressed for no reason at all...
Sometimes I wish I were on top of the Sears Towers and just fall...

I wish I know why I felt this way,
But I know the Lord will help me find out one day.

This feeling that I get isn't very cool,
B-cuz it may come while I'm on the bus, or even at school.

I really want to know; why do I feel all this heart-ache and pain...
Maybe it's because I have parents on Heroin or Cocaine.

It really hurts me to write these things, that's so very bold.
But I have to get it out one way or another, cause if I don't I might just explode.

I'm broke as hell and I don't have no money,
Because these shady ass jobs won't call on me.

I wonder why the Lord picked this terrible life for me,
But I bet he did it for a reason, just wait one day, I'll see.

242

Maybe it's for the better or maybe it's for the worst.
Maybe in college, from my family, I'll be the first.

Some of these things I say are in the line of danger,
I know what I'm saying is coming from depression and anger.

All I have to do is stay strong and survive,
But with God on my side, I know I'll survive.

If things don't get under control,
I think I'm liable to slit my wrist with a knife.
But I know what risk I'm taking...
It's my life.

Written 11/13/95 at 11:31 p.m.
By: LaTanya LaTrice Beasley

My Life with Uncle Bobby

I was sixteen when I wrote the poem *My Life*. I didn't have a therapist or anyone to sit me down and ask, "What's going on inside you?" I didn't have that kind of support at home or anywhere else.
Writing was my release. It was my therapy before I even knew what therapy was.

When we moved out of that dark basement apartment, I thought things might get better. But a new house doesn't fix old pain.

I was still tired of seeing my mama and her boyfriend get high behind that closed bedroom door like it was normal. I was tired of strangers walking in and out of our home like they paid rent. I was also tired of being a kid who knew in her gut: *my mama is a dope fiend.*

That poem wasn't written for attention. It was written because I didn't know what else to do. I wasn't trying to die, not really, but at the time I didn't care whether I lived or not. I didn't have a plan or the courage to take my own life.

But I did have questions. I spent more time wondering how people could take their lives than actually planning to take my own.

Even with all the death I had written about, somewhere deep down, buried under all that sadness, I still believed God had something better for me.

It's strange how you can feel two things at once: hopeless and determined. Broken and still showing up.
I still danced. I still smiled. I was in social groups and dance

groups. At CVS, I was popular.

Nobody knew I went home and cried alone. Nobody knew I left my shame at the door of that school building, only to pick it back up the second I stepped back inside my house.

But then, loss has a way of pulling the mask off.

When my Uncle Bobby died, something in me felt really sad, afraid, and broken.

Uncle Bobby was one of the few people who really talked to me. He was always a protector of the women in his life. He gave me advice and saw past my jokes, past my dance routines, past the fake confidence. He talked to me, made broken promises, made me laugh, he was always honest with me about life, and wanted me to make good choices.

He knew I was more than the chaos I came from, the chaos our family often gave me, and the chaos in my home. One day he was here and just like that, he was gone.

He had been living in our basement apartment with us while he was getting clean. He was reading his Bible, going to church, and going to AA meetings. He was really trying to stay sober. My mom was still using, right there under the same roof, but he stuck to his plan.

The last time I saw him alive, I had just come home from a cheer competition, excited to have won third place. I was proud and glowing.

He was getting dressed to go out to an AA social at a local sobriety club around our house, sharp in his gray slacks and that alligator print shirt. He was excited to show us the new outfit he'd purchased for the event.

I told him he looked nice. Me and my friends hyped him up about his outfit. I remember how hard he smiled. And that was the last smile I ever got from him.

At the end of the day, I realized he didn't come home. I told my mom, "Uncle Bobby must be having a good time." We both laughed.

A few hours later, my mom came into my room. Her eyes were glassy, her words heavy.

"Granny just called. Uncle Bobby called her and said he messed up. He spent his whole check. He said he's tired of disappointing them. He said he's going to take his life."

Then she looked at me, as if I could answer the impossible. "You think he's really going to do it?"

We both looked at each other and said, "No way."
And I went to sleep.

The next day at school, my cousin and I got pulled from class. My cousin by my side. My aunt stood there in her house shoes, messy hair, harboring hurt and heartbreak.

We walked into the office and my aunt stood up and immediately embraced us.
"Y'all... Uncle Bobby is dead."

Just like that, I remembered the conversation my mom and I had the night before

Turned out my uncle really did the unthinkable.

He jumped from the 79th Street bridge onto the expressway below.

For years, I didn't even want to go by that bridge.

Sometimes, crossing it now, I still think about the day his relapse made him climb that fence and let go.

I didn't tell anyone how deep his death cut me. No one even asked. Not my friends, not my teachers, not even my mama.

I just carried it. Like I carried everything else.

I knew how hard he tried to stay sober.
I saw his efforts. I saw him reading his Bible, listening to sermons on cassette tapes, doing his best to hold on.

I still remember him in that sharp outfit, Kool-Aid smile and all, on his way to a sober party. To know that something happened there, or after, that made him relapse and take his life... I was devastated.

But I hid it well.

I kept dancing, kept laughing, kept moving. When it started to hurt, I wrote.

From his death, I realized the dangers of drugs from a different perspective.
I also remembered what he told me:

"Weed is a gateway drug. If you smoke weed and get addicted, your tolerance builds up and you graduate to the next hard drug. Your mom, Uncle D, and all of us, graduated. Don't be like us."

I heard exactly what he said.
But it took me time to truly listen.

The Test I Almost Failed In My Life

In My Life I wrote:

I'm broke as hell and I don't have no money,
Because these shady ass jobs won't call on me.

When I finally got my first opportunity for a job, I was immediately hit was a test.

Life is always full of tests. Some tests are presented for us to pass or fail. Some are there to test our physical or mental strength. And some are placed in your path to shape your future.

There's a particular test I can't forget. Not because it's the worst test I had, not that I failed it, but because it taught me who I didn't want to become.

It happened right before I got the job at Jewel. I landed the interview because my friend hooked me up. She already worked there and told me it was in the bag. The manager loved her and trusted her. I was so excited. Finally, my first real job. A step toward something better.

More importantly, finally a break away from my mom's once per month check.

Me and my friend went to the store on a Friday directly after school. I met the store manager and the official interview was scheduled for the following Tuesday. When we left the store, she wanted to celebrate.

"Let's smoke," she said.

I had smoked a few times before, but I wasn't into drugs. I didn't like being high or out of my body. But she didn't want to smoke alone, and I didn't want to kill her vibe. So, I said yes. Peer pressure isn't always loud. Sometimes it's just stupid, quiet loyalty.

We walked through the alleys between seventy-sixth and seventy-eighth. The cracked concrete, the garage doors tagged with graffiti, the stinky garbage spilling out of black bins, and the smell of urine filled the air and stained the sidewalk. I was still there, walking through it all, smoking a blunt I hadn't planned to touch.

Before we lit it, I asked her several times if Jewel required a drug test. She laughed at how paranoid I was being and told me they didn't. She was confident. I was naïve.

That Tuesday, I showed up ready to slay the interview. I had my bootleg Résumé printed. I had my crooked smile in place and my confidence didn't show my fear. The interview turned out to be a general conversation about the job and how I will start on the front-end as a bagger. Then the manager hit me with, "Ms. Beasley, it's been a pleasure. We're happy to have you on board. You just need a passed drug test."

I felt like I was about to pass out. I couldn't believe what I was hearing.

I was sick and mad. Not at her, but at myself. I gave in and did something I didn't even enjoy. After everything my uncle told me, after everything I had seen drugs do in my life, I should have known better.

I was worried I had blown my chance. I knew exactly who could help, my mom. She was a professional at getting past drug tests. I told my mom I had been around people who were smoking. I left out the part where I was the one holding and hitting the blunt. She didn't yell. She gave me a plan.

I knew she'd know exactly what to do. I had given her my pee a few times before. I'd even watched her put crazy glue on her fingerprints to get past job screenings.

Her instructions were simple.

"Get clean pee from somebody else. Put it in a condom. Keep it warm between your legs. Have a safety pin somewhere on you so you can poke it and pour it out. The warmth is important to match your body temp. If the temperature is not right, you will automatically fail."

She even had me practice with water in a condom the night before. All I could think was, *this lady is a pro at this.*

The day of the test, my friend Cheryl drove me there. I decided it was better to get her pee right before the test to ensure it stayed warm.

We stopped at the McDonald's on 83rd and Ashland. I stood in line, grabbed a courtesy cup of water and an apple pie. Then we headed to the bathroom to execute the plan.

That bathroom was nasty. The stalls were marked up with graffiti. The air smelled fishy. The toilets were dirty, and we did everything to avoid touching anything. Still, I had to get it done.

In the stall, my friend peed into the flimsy courtesy cup. She came out holding it like she didn't want any part of her own urine. Over the sink, I held the condom open with my bare hands while she poured it in, no gloves in site, like we were doing some twisted science experiment.

Once it was full, I tied it up and tucked it down into my underwear. It was warm and hidden, and I was completely disgusted by the warmth.

I sat cross-legged in the car as we drove across the street, pretending I wasn't carrying someone else's pee between my thighs.

At the clinic, I walked in like I was just another honest young girl about to pass her test. When I got to the back, the nurse gave me the usual rules: pee in this cup, when you're done, no flushing, no washing your hands, and you must keep the door cracked.

I had practiced. Now it was time to execute.

In the restroom I slipped the safety pin from under my shirt, poked a hole in the condom, and poured the urine into the cup. It was still warm. The temperature was perfect.

But there was one problem. There was no trash can in the bathroom. I couldn't flush the toilet. There was nowhere to hide the evidence.

So, I wrapped the condom in a bunch of tissue, slid it back into my bottoms, and walked out like nothing happened.

Later, when the nurse stepped out with my "specimen," I reached down, tossed it in the trash and acted like I had nothing to hide.

After a few days of feeling ashamed and nervous, I finally received the call. I passed... well my Cheryl passed the drug test. I got the job.

But something about that day stuck with me.

Between the urine smell, the bathroom, and the graffiti on the walls, I made a life-long decision.

Never again will I smoke weed or put myself in such a crazy situation.

Not because somebody warned me. Not because of Uncle Bobby's death. Not even because of my mama.

It was because I had seen, with my own eyes, how drugs...even weed, even... "just a blunt" can lead you into places you never expected to be. Drugs can make you compromise yourself without even thinking about the cost.

It wasn't really about the weed. It was about my shame and my choices.

That day, with that condom, that lie, and that disgust... I hit my breaking point.

That was my enough-is-enough.

A Short Reflection Of My Life

I think back to the girl who wrote *My Life* and I see now:
I wasn't just writing about wanting to die. I was writing about wanting to live, but not knowing how. I was writing my way toward survival and my way to freedom.

And though my mama was hooked on heroin, and though my father barely showed up, and though I spent years picking up pieces other people shattered, I still made my own choices. Not perfect ones, but they were mine.

Today, I can say with my whole chest: I am more than a dope fiend's daughter. I own my own story. I own my own life.

My Life With Ray, My Father

My father was always around, in his own way. And in our own way, we had a beautiful relationship.

I started calling him "I'mma Do" because he was always talking about what he was going to do. "I'mma do this." "I'mma do that." But between his addiction to drugs and alcohol, most of those plans stayed words. Still, I never held that against him.

From the time I learned to talk, I never called him "Dad." I called him Ray. Not out of disrespect. I just heard everyone else call him by his name, and he never corrected me. That's simply what stuck.

Ray was stubborn. He cursed like a sailor. He marched to the beat of his own drum and didn't care if anyone else heard the rhythm. But he was present in the way he knew how to be.

Growing up, I remember all the times we moved, and I remember my father always visiting. Sometimes he hung around with my mother and whoever she was dating at the time. Other times he was just spending time with me or taking me to the store.

Looking back, it felt normal to have him around. Whether he was there to see me or to get high, I'll never truly know. But what I do know is that my mother and Ray always had a respectful relationship.

Ray didn't care who was around when he wanted to spend time with me, and the men in my mother's life always respected his presence.

Years later, when my mother co-authored a book, I learned more about their past. My parents got together when my mother was deep in her addiction and my father was the supplier. At some point, there was abuse between them, but in time, they reconciled.

Whatever pain existed back then, they found a way to leave it behind. By the time I was old enough to understand their dynamic, their relationship had settled into mutual respect.

After my mother's sobriety, my father always had love for her. Not in a romantic way, but more like a friend. He respected her deeply for the way she carried herself, for the strength it took to overcome an addiction he still struggled with, and for how she only ever looked back to help someone else up, including him.

In 2003, my father moved to Jackson, Tennessee, and detoxed from heroin. He still drank his beer and sometimes dark liquor, but he stayed off drugs.

Whenever I could help, I did. I supported him financially when he needed it and even added him to my phone line so we could stay in touch.

In 2013, he was approved for SSI benefits and finally got Section 8 housing. For the first time in my adult life, I felt proud of him. Not because SSI and Section 8 housing was an accomplishment. It was because he had something of his own. He got new dentures, new glasses, new furniture. Small things to others, but big to me.

They meant security and dignity. He was happy to be in his own space and out of everyone else's way. He paid his rent and kept his place clean... until he couldn't.

One night in 2017, he called me, sad and embarrassed. I could hear the shame in his voice. He told me he had fallen off the wagon and didn't know how it happened.

During the call, I remember wondering why he was even on a wagon. Then I got it.

After fourteen years of not using heroin, he had relapsed.

I kept my composure on the phone. I listened and didn't judge. Just like I did when I saw him in jail, I cried after we hung up.

Hearing those words made me feel like a kid again. I felt sad for my father. I felt powerless and scared. I was just wishing things could be different.

He lost the small things he had worked: for his apartment, his sense of peace. I was heartbroken, but I wasn't angry. I understood the battle he was fighting.

A few months later, he asked for money here and there. I sent it to him. One day, he asked for fifty dollars and sent his cousin to my house to get it. His cousin told me this was the last time he was doing that for Ray. I was confused on why it was his last time coming to get money from me. He made note that it was too dangerous.

That's when I understood why his cousin said "doing that". That is why he was so uptight about what Ray was asking.

Basically, my father had me to give him money so his cousin could get him drugs and send it to him in Tennessee.

I was not happy. I called him and told him I loved him, but that was where I drew the line. I hated drugs. And I couldn't be an enabler.

He felt bad afterward and didn't call for months.

The next time we talked, my tone was a little softer. Our conversation was better.

In January 2018, I got engaged. I called him the next day, full of excitement. He told me that when he saw the photos on social media, it hit him like a ton of bricks. He knew what came next.

I told him I loved him and wanted him at my wedding, but not as an addict. I couldn't let him walk me down the aisle in that condition.

He didn't give excuses. He understood.

The next day, he checked himself into rehab to detox. But Ray, being Ray, he signed himself out. He told me he didn't like how the staff treated the patients. He said the staff didn't treat anyone with respect, they spoke down on them, and their tone was disrespectful.

I knew Ray didn't like being told what to do, especially by people with the wrong tone. I remembered the stories of how he got in trouble while he was enlisted in the US Marine Corp. While in the

Marines when he was told something like "Dotson, drop down and give me fifty push-ups," Ray would respond by saying "I ain't giving you shit." Needless to say, his time in the Marines didn't end honorably.

That was just who he was. In some ways, those traits were passed down to me. In all his strong-headed and stubborn ways he always listened to me. He always asked me for advice and my opinion mattered to him.

Despite how stubborn he was and how many times life knocked him down, my father loved me enough to try again. And that was enough for me.

Soon after, he found an outpatient program. They gave him Suboxone to help him stay clean. Eventually, he weaned himself off that too.

On May 25, 2019, I got married. My father was there. Fully present. Sober. Smiling as he walked me down the aisle.

That day will always be one of my greatest gifts.

He and my aunt stayed at my house with my kids while I went on my honeymoon. On June 1, 2019, he left to go back home; that was his last visit to Chicago.

In early 2021, my father tried hard to come back to Chicago to visit me and my kids. He kept saying he had to see us. That he missed us deeply. Something in his voice told me he meant it more than ever before.

Then, the day after Mother's Day, everything changed.

He fell ill and was found unresponsive by one of his sisters. He was rushed to the hospital and ended up in the ICU, where he stayed for months. I flew down a few times to be by his side. But each time I arrived, he was in a medically induced coma. And every time I saw him like that... silent, restrained, unreachable... something inside me broke a little more.

There's only one hospital in Jackson, Tennessee. While they managed to revive him, the care he received afterward was a different story. It was heartbreaking. They fed him a rotation of psychotropic drugs like he was a test subject. One day it was something for anxiety. The next, for schizophrenia. Then something else. He had restraints on his hands and feet for two whole months.

When they finally weaned him off the ventilator, he still couldn't return to his right mind. He was disoriented. Lost. At one point, they even considered discharging him to a psych ward.

Go figure.

Any sane person would go crazy under that kind of treatment.

The entire two-month stretch was emotionally draining. I cried every single day. Not just because I saw my father suffering, but because it felt like no one was fighting for him. They weren't trying to bring him back. They were trying to keep him down.

My aunt, who lives in Tennessee, visited him daily. She never missed a day. No matter how much hell Ray raised in life, no matter how many times he cursed out his siblings, they still showed up. They still loved him.

But he never recovered.

On July 18, 2021, while I was on the phone with my aunt, my father took his last breath. I told him I loved him and it hurt me knowing that would be the last time he'd hear my words. I am grateful that he was surrounded by all his brothers and sisters. Many of them he had pushed away at some point... but they were there.

It was just two days after my mother celebrated 23 years of sobriety.

I used to think I didn't want to be in the room when someone I loved passed. But in that moment, I wished I had been. I wished I could have held his hand. Whispered something into his ear. Just been there.

But God saw fit otherwise.

With the help of my family, I laid him to rest with dignity in Chicago. He was eulogized by a childhood friend, everything was perfect. I was also grateful to have my mother stand right beside me.

Today, I have peace knowing he's no longer suffering. But I'm still learning how to make peace with the way he spent his final days... restrained, drugged, and misunderstood. When I cry now, I cry for me. Not for him.

Because he's finally free.

My story is written exactly how I lived it. My mother raised me. My father didn't raise me in the traditional sense, but he was present in his own way and I accepted him for who he was.

Just like my aunt and grandmother stepped in for me, I stepped in for my sister, who was born in 1997. Her mother passed in 1998, and my father wasn't stable enough to raise her.

She was raised by her older sister, but I kept her for Christmas breaks and summer vacations. Over the years, I helped however I could because I knew what it meant to be the child left behind.

Ray wasn't a traditional father. He didn't directly teach us about life, but we learned a lot from him. While I made peace with his role in my life, his dependency and addiction kept him from being who my sister needed him to be. We knew that he loved us both deeply. We were his pride and joy, as he often said.

I accepted my relationship with my father for what it was: imperfect, unconventional, but rooted in love. To this day, people still say to me:

"Tanya, you know your dad loved you and your sister."
"Tanya, your dad was so proud of you."

After he died, a friend told me how serious he was about getting clean for my wedding. He was at her house when we spoke after I got engaged. He told her that I wanted him to be present at my wedding, and that he wouldn't miss that moment for the world. It's those stories that make me miss him dearly.

His life taught me this: people don't have to show up perfectly to deserve or show love. They don't have to get everything right to still matter.

Sometimes, the people we love can only meet us halfway. We have to decide if halfway is enough for us to hold onto.

For me, it was.

Having my father walk me down the aisle sober wasn't just about the wedding. It was about the little girl in me finally seeing him keep a promise...not with words, but with action.

It was about knowing that, just for that day, he showed up as his best self. I got to carry that memory with pride, not pain.

I miss him. I miss him every day. But I've made peace with the man he was and the man he couldn't always be.

His life taught me about grace, acceptance, and loving people where they are...not where we wish they were.

Our relationship wasn't perfect or traditional. But it worked for us.

And for that, I will always be grateful.

Because of him, I learned how to love others; and myself, with more grace.

God In My Life

When I wrote *My Life*, I didn't know it was more than just a poem. I didn't know it would become a mirror, a reminder of how far I'd come. Back then, I was just trying to survive my emotions. Now I understand how every experience, every heartbreak, and every choice led me to healing, clarity, and faith.

I wrote, *"I wonder why God chose such a terrible life for me. I will know one day. I'll see."*

In retrospect, I see it clearly.

The life I once saw as terrible is now my living testimony. My life turned out to be amazing. Even when things aren't as favorable as I'd like, my life still holds balance.

Back then, I didn't have the strongest relationship with God, but I knew there was a higher power who could not only bless me but turn my life around.

One Easter Sunday stands out more clearly than most.

My cousin Michelle and I got up bright and early. We were excited to follow through with the plan we'd made for ourselves. No Easter baskets in sight, just clothes we already had in our wardrobes. We were up before anyone else in the house. The only adult was still asleep.

We quietly walked out of the house to carry out our plan.

From my aunt's house on 17th Avenue, we walked just four blocks to Broadview Baptist Church. At that time, the church sat humbly a few blocks down the same street. A light-colored brick building with modest stained-glass windows, worn concrete steps, and church doors that welcomed anyone who entered.

We were just two unsupervised kids making decisions for ourselves. Michelle was about fifteen, and I was around eleven. We walked through quiet suburban streets in our Sunday best. Our shoes were simple, our socks had little ruffles, but we didn't care.

We found a spot near the middle of the pews and slid in quietly beside people we didn't know. The pew cushions were stiff, and the air carried that familiar scent of polished wood and worn-out Bibles. We sat with our hands in our laps, legs swinging a little, trying to blend in, but proud that we made it there on our own.

She was ready to hear a word. I was ready to see the choir march in through the sanctuary doors, singing in their robes until they took their seats behind the pulpit.

We didn't go to church because someone made us. We weren't there to impress anyone. We were there because we needed to be.

At the end of the service, when the pastor called for new members to come forward, my cousin stood up.

I was confused. Joining was not part of the plan. I looked at her like, *"Girl, what are you doing?"* But as always, I followed her.

I felt silly standing up there, like we were pretending to be somebody's grown children. I half-way expected someone to tap me on the shoulder and ask, *"Baby, where's your mama?"*

Nobody tapped me. They just kept clapping.

And there we were. Standing up front with the other new members like we had any business being up there. I didn't know whether to laugh, cry, or sneak out the side door before they noticed how young we were and that we were unsupervised.

But something about it felt good; safe, even.

When we made our way to the front, the church clapped for us. Not loud and rowdy, but a warm, steady, welcoming applause that wrapped around us like a blessing. I didn't know why it felt so good, but it did.

That was the Easter we joined the church.

Looking back, I wonder if she knew what she was doing. Reaching for something greater. Maybe something more stable.

For me, I didn't fully understand. My Granny had taken us to church at Mission of Faith quite often, and I visited my great-uncle's apostolic church on 63rd and Vernon from time to time. But it had been a while since I'd seen the inside of a church.

What were we doing there without our parents?

We were doing what God led us to do. Whether knowingly on her part or unknowingly on mine, we were there.

I remember when we went to the back to fill out information cards. They asked if we wanted to be baptized.

Still confused, I turned to Michelle to see what she would say. She said yes. So, I said yes.

She knew what baptism meant. I just knew people were dipped in water at church, with the preacher's hand over their face, that's it.

Even then, I remember thinking, *"I don't think we supposed to be doing this without a grown-up."* But we did it anyway. We filled out those cards like we were signing up for summer camp.

Looking back, I still laugh at how bold we were.

About two weeks later, I was back at my aunt's house. Our parents had gotten us everything we needed to be baptized: a swimming cap, a white sheet, a change of clothes.

But the courage to follow through... that came from us.

That Sunday morning, we woke up, got dressed, packed our plastic bags, and walked back up to the church.

Michelle and I were baptized at Broadview Baptist Church.

No mother. No aunt. No adult from our family. Just us and our faith.

Two unsupervised minors, knowingly or not realizing reaching for God through our parents' absence.

Here's the funny part: after all that, I never went back to that church again. Not once. I can't tell you what happened to that congregation, who the pastor was, or what Sunday service looked like afterward.

We walked in boldly, left baptized, and honestly, that was the end of my story with that church.

But years later, I look back on that moment not as something small, but as something brave. A seed planted in faith that helped shape who I became.

Even then, without knowing fully why, I understood one thing: God had me.

Back then, I thought baptism was just water and tradition. But now I understand it as protection. As belonging. As a promise I made to myself and to God, even when the rest of my life felt unsure.

That moment taught me that faith doesn't always need witnesses to be real. Sometimes it only needs two little girls, a plan, a nearby church, and a confused yes."

A Busy Life

When I was younger, I always found ways to stay busy and follow my passions. I joined dance groups, usually signing myself up, sometimes with a friend. I'd take the bus to try out and hope I had enough money to make it to future practices.

I remember the summers I spent dancing with U-Phi-U, one of the most popular dance groups in Chicago during the '90s. In Chicago, one of the biggest highlights of the summer was performing in the Bud Billiken Parade.

That parade ran from 31st to 55th on King Drive. The parade was an opportunity to be seen by many, to be on TV, and to show off new routines.

I practiced all summer long in the sweltering heat. Sweating through routines, perfecting moves, and hoping for my moment.

But not having the money for a parade uniform meant I couldn't perform; not just in the parade, but at performances for months afterward.

It was humiliating to show up, work hard, be placed in the routine, and then have to sit on the sidelines because I couldn't afford the uniform.

Eventually, I started telling my Aunt Cil, my father's sister, or my Granny how it felt to be left out. How it felt to have all my time and efforts go to waste.

When I opened up, they helped me get what I needed.

From the gym at Jackson Park Fieldhouse to the stage at the Regal Theater, I had many performances. No one from my family came to see me. No one was there to cheer me on.

But I didn't care.

As long as I was dancing, doing something I loved, that was enough.

I also signed myself up for Windy City All Stars, a competitive cheer team in the '90s. I had no idea at the time how expensive that was for "normal" families.

But the coach let me practice with the team two to three times a week without ever asking for a dime.

He taught me how to tumble. He taught me to cheer. And he never treated me any different than the other girls.

When it was time to perform or compete, he made sure I had a uniform too.

Back then, I was just following my heart. I'd seen the team at a competition and was in awe. So, I tracked down where they practiced, showed up at the park, talked to the coach, and he let me join.

Years later, when my daughter Trinity was younger, I enrolled her in an All-Star cheerleading program. That's when I realized just how expensive it really was.

I also saw how involved a parent had to be. And that made me reflect; I had been that committed, that present, making it to the practices on the bus without any parent at all.

Looking back now, I see how that coach became a part of the balance God gave me.

He didn't know why my mom wasn't there. He just saw a kid with drive, a kid who showed up with heart.

And once again, that was nobody but God.

How Writing Shaped My Life

The poem *My Life* was special for many reasons.

Throughout my life, I'd written plenty of poems. Writing was how I let things out in a creative way, especially when I couldn't fully express myself verbally.

In my sophomore year, I wrote a series of poems about drugs and how they affect families and children. Without telling us, my teacher entered them into a citywide competition.

To me, it was no big deal. I wasn't even using my real name. I signed them "Ton-Ton," the nickname given to me by my father's side of the family.

The teacher didn't check to make sure my real name was on them. I didn't think anyone would care much about what I wrote anyway.

But the following week, she came back to class furious. My poetry about my crazy, chaotic, drug-filled life had won not just one award but several special mentions.

She showed up with the ribbons and trophies. But she never gave them to me., because I hadn't put my name on the work.

That moment taught me something:

She didn't take accountability. She blamed me for something she should've double-checked before submitting.

But more importantly, I learned this:

Keep your work. Put your name on it. Own your story.

The poem *My Life* was no different.

Thirty years later, I had no idea that same poem would still be with me. That it would become part of something bigger… and still matter.

I kept it for a reason.

That poem opened the door to my first therapy visit. That visit led to questions about my first memory of my mom using drugs. And those answers eventually led to this memoir.

Looking back, I see exactly why I held on to it.

To read it again later.
To reflect.
To understand how it would all come full circle.
To see God's glory in my story.

At sixteen, I was writing to vent. I didn't know I was also writing prophecy. Even in the darkness, I believed there would be light.

That poem wasn't just words scribbled in a notebook. It became a thread tying together the girl I was, the woman I became, and the writer I am now.

My Life in College and Beyond

In *My Life*, I also wrote:
"Maybe it's for the better, maybe it's for the worst. Maybe in college, from my family, I'll be the first."

Looking back, in 1995, no one in my immediate family had a college degree. Today, that story has changed. Many of my cousins hold multiple degrees, and most importantly, my mom earned hers too.

When I graduated high school, I really wanted to go away to college. But I didn't. I didn't want to rely on my mother or anyone else to help me get by. Getting to and from CVS High School had already been hard enough. The idea of being far from home without even the basics made me hesitate.

So I enrolled at Harold Washington College for a few semesters, then eventually dropped out in 2000 to work full-time.

I landed jobs with reputable organizations and made enough to afford a stable life with nice things. Still, I couldn't shake the feeling that I wasn't finished. There was more in me.

In December 2009, I went on my first date with my now husband. In hindsight back then, he was just a guy I was still trying to figure out, he wasn't really the type of guy I'd dated in the past. In the past I was always attracted to drug dealers and dope boys. By the time we met I matured a lot, so I also wanted to move away from "street guys" for obvious reasons. It was cold, typical Chicago winter cold, and we were driving down Lake Shore Drive near Soldier Field. We were headed to Lucky Strike to grab a bite to eat and catch a basketball game at the sports bar.

I was thinking we'd talk about the usual stuff like jobs, music, favorite foods, maybe even have conversations about his favorite color. But no… Out of nowhere, he hit me with, "So what do you want to do in the next five years?"

I stared at him like, "Excuse me, sir?" I was not ready for an Oprah Super Soul Sunday interview or a Ted Talk over wings and a game. I expected small talk. Maybe a laugh or two. Not a life-planning session.

Still, I answered. I told him some things I'd thought about but hadn't actually done yet. I mentioned going back to school, even though I didn't really have a plan. I spoke about how I loved writing. At the time, I also had this dream of writing a book. I didn't know how, but it was floating around in my head.

I wasn't super polished about it, and I definitely didn't have a five-year timeline mapped out. But I said it. And honestly, saying it out loud made it feel a little more real.

The following month he kept asking me if I was going to enroll. I didn't want him to keep asking me without action. In January 2010, I stopped procrastinating and decided to go back to school. I re-enrolled at the City Colleges of Chicago and earned my Associate of Arts degree in 2014. After that, in 2016, I obtained my Bachelor of Arts in Organizational Leadership from Roosevelt University.

But the degree itself wasn't my proudest accomplishment.

The real victory was this: I was able to follow in the footsteps of someone I once couldn't follow anywhere.

My mother, who had once been lost in her addiction, had become someone I could finally look to as an example. Her path helped light my own.

For a long time, I lived my life determined to do everything opposite of my parents. Every choice and every plan was about not repeating their mistakes.

Even when I went back to school, I was proud. Not because I was doing it despite my mother, but because I was finally doing something positive to follow in her footsteps.

In 2019, I parted ways with a company where I had worked for fifteen years. I didn't step out on faith...I was forced; but, I stayed out on faith.

And staying out meant I was unemployed during COVID.

That was new for me. I had been working since I was seventeen. I didn't know what it felt like to be still and finally own my life without the terms or schedule of anyone else.

During COVID, everything stopped. No activities. No distractions. Just me, my family, and my thoughts.

That's when I realized something important:
Outside of doing everything differently than my parents, I didn't know what I wanted. Not in reaction to their past, but because of who I am.

That season forced me to slow down and ask real questions. What do I want for my life? What do I want for my future?

It wasn't easy. I hadn't realized how much their pain had shaped my decisions.

But in that stillness, I turned my hobby of making shirts into an actual business, Beasiley Created (be easily created). The name was based on my ease of creating nice things. The was also during the same time, *The Diary of a Dope Fiend's Daughter* was conceptualized.

It started as just a book idea. I kept procrastinating because I wasn't sure my story could help anyone.

But through prayer and meditation, the vision became clearer.

This wasn't just a book. It needed to be a space where others could write their truth, the way I wrote mine.

My prayer with this project is simple:
To help people find their voices, even if it's just a quiet one, shared with no one.

And my bigger prayer is this:
To help heal families broken by substance abuse, one story, one pen, one pencil, one chapter at a time.

Because it takes courage to let out what you've been holding in for too long.

I am LaTanya Beasley-Carter.
I am the adult child of two recovered dope fiends.
This is my story.
This is my diary.
And *My Life* was just the beginning.

Truth Be Told

Truth be told, I used to think My Life was something I needed to escape.
Something I had to fix or completely rewrite.

But I see it differently now.
I see how every hard place had a lesson.
How every person who failed me still taught me something.
How even the outlet of writing shaped my voice.

My Life didn't break me, it built me.
Not all at once. Literally, not without ugly scars.
But slowly, truthfully, and with grace.

The girl who wrote that poem was reaching for freedom without knowing what it looked like.
And now, I can say: freedom looks like ownership.
It looks like owning your truth.
It looks like peace, even with a chaotic past.

I don't owe shame or silence anything.
What I owe is honor: to the girl I was, the woman I became, and the God who never left me in between.

And so, truth be told...
My Life didn't go the way I planned.
But somehow, it became everything I needed.

LET'S DO THE HEART WORK:
My Life

You've made it to the end of my story, but maybe you're just beginning to meet your own in a new way. Take a breath here. Reflect gently. There is no rush to arrive, no pressure to heal it all at once. All that matters is that you showed up, and you're still showing up now.

The Heart Work For
Everyone Who Wants to Heal

Now that you've walked through these pages, what story are you ready to stop hiding from, and what part of your story are you finally ready to live out loud?

BREATH BREAK BEFORE YOU CONTINUE

Before moving into your final chapter or reflection, take a **Breath Break** to honor your body and spirit:

- Sit comfortably and place one hand on your heart, one hand on your belly.
- Inhale deeply through your nose for a count of 4, hold for a count of 4, and exhale slowly through your mouth for a count of 6.
- As you breathe, say quietly to yourself: *"I am safe. I am allowed to rest. I am allowed to heal."*
- Repeat this breathing cycle three times, letting your shoulders drop with each exhale.
- Allow yourself to notice any tension you are holding and give yourself permission to release it.

When you are ready, thank yourself for showing up to your heart work, and continue your journey at your own gentle pace.

CHAPTER ELEVEN:
The Glory In Your Story

You've come this far through my pain, healing, and growth. Now it's time for yours.

This final chapter isn't about me, my mom, my dad, or my past... it's all about you.
Your silence deserves sound.
Your wounds deserve room to be treated and healed.
Your story deserves to be told in your own way, in your own space.

You deserve the glory in your story.
Not just the kind that shows up in success, but the kind that shows up when you speak up.
The kind that shows up when you speak the truth, even if your voice trembles.
The kind that shows up when you look back and finally say, *"I didn't deserve that... but I do deserve to heal.."*

So, this is your space. I want you to write it, scribble it, speak it. shout it, or whisper it.
But whatever you do, don't bury it.

This space is yours now.
Because your story has glory too.
And this time, the pen is in your hand.

FINAL NOTE FROM THE AUTHOR

If you've made it to the end of this book, thank you. Thank you for holding space for my truth. Thank you for being willing to witness pain, joy, shame, growth, and healing all in one journey.

This book was never just about my story. It was a mirror for the stories so many of us carry. Our stories are like a secret society of survivor's people only hear about if someone else is brave enough to talk.

My prayer is that *The Diary of a Dope Fiend's Daughter* reminded you that healing is not linear, and neither is love. That it showed you how strength comes out of our weaknesses. That you saw that even when it's messy and hard, your life still has purpose.

Healing begins when you make up in your mind that you're ready.

If reading this stirred something in you, whether it brought tears, questions, or clarity, I hope you'll take the next brave step. Whether it's journaling, calling someone, finding a therapist, or simply resting, please remember: **you are not alone**.

I am looking forward to hearing how this project set you free!

Keep writing. Keep choosing yourself. And keep walking toward the version of you that is whole, free, and deeply loved.

With grace,
LaTanya Beasley-Carter

HEALING BEYOND THIS BOOK

If this book stirred something deep or reopened old wounds, know this: you don't have to carry it alone. Below are a few resources that may offer support, connection, and a path forward.

Mental Health & Crisis Support

988 Suicide & Crisis Lifeline
Call 988 (U.S., 24/7) for confidential support.
Website: 988lifeline.org

Veterans Crisis Line
Call 988 and press 1 for veteran-specific support.
Website: veteranscrisisline.net

Crisis Text Line
Text HOME to 741741 (or STEVE if you're a young person of color) for 24/7 support.
Website: crisistextline.org

SAMHSA National Helpline
Call 1-800-662-HELP (4357) for free, confidential support and treatment referrals.
Website: samhsa.gov

THERAPY & COUNSELING RESOURCES

Therapy for Black Girls
Online therapist directory and podcast.
Website: therapyforblackgirls.com

Open Path Collective
Affordable in-person and online therapy ($30–$60/session).
Website: openpathcollective.org

TMH Behavioral Services
Licensed mental health practice in Illinois and Texas
Website: www.tmhbehavioralservices.com

Growing Boundlessly
Licensed mental health practice in Illinois, Indiana, Texas, and Michigan
Website: www.growingboundlessly.com

SUBSTANCE ABUSE & RECOVERY

Alcoholics Anonymous (AA) and Narcotics Anonymous (NA)
Peer-led support groups nationwide.
Websites:
aa.org
na.org

Al-Anon & Alateen
Support for families and children affected by addiction.
Website: al-anon.org

FindTreatment.gov (SAMHSA Treatment Locator)
Search treatment centers by ZIP code.
Website: findtreatment.gov

SUPPORT FOR CHILDREN OF ADDICTED PARENTS

National Association for Children of Addiction (NACoA)
Resources, education, and support.
Website: nacoa.org

Adult Children of Alcoholics/Dysfunctional Families (ACA)
12-step program and meeting locator.
Website: adultchildren.org

FAITH-BASED AND SPIRITUAL SUPPORT

The Confess Project
Mental health advocacy for men of color.
Website: theconfessproject.com

Local Churches and Ministries
Many offer free spiritual counseling or recovery ministries. Look for those aligned with your values.

LGBTQ+ YOUTH SUPPORT

The Trevor Project
Crisis intervention and suicide prevention for LGBTQ+ youth.
Website: thetrevorproject.org

Trans Lifeline
Peer support and crisis hotline for trans people.
Website: translifeline.org

Center on Halsted (Chicago)
LGBTQ+ community center offering youth and mental health support.
Website: centeronhalsted.org

ADDITIONAL NATIONAL HELPLINES (U.S.)

National Runaway Safeline
Call 1-800-RUNAWAY (1-800-786-2929)
Website: 1800runaway.org

2-1-1 Helpline
Dial 211 for access to local support services like housing, food, and counseling.
Website: 211.org

www.ingramcontent.com/pod-product-compliance
Lightning Source LLC
Chambersburg PA
CBHW042315120626
46547CB00022B/2016